PUNCHNEEDLE EMBROIDERY

Dancing Needles

PUNCHNEEDLE EMBROIDERY

Dancing Needles

PAMELA GURNEY

SALLYMILNER
PUBLISHING

First published in 2003 by
Sally Milner Publishing Pty Ltd
PO Box 2104
Bowral NSW 2576
AUSTRALIA

© Pamela Gurney 2003
Reprinted 2004, 2005, 2006

Design: Anna Warren, Warren Ventures Pty Ltd
Editing: Anne Savage
Photography: Tim Connolly

Printed in China

National Library of Australia Cataloguing-in-Publication data:

    Gurney, Pamela.
    Punchneedle embroidery.

    ISBN 1 86351 313 2.

    1. Embroidery. 2. Punched work. I. Title. (Series :
    Milner craft series).

    746.44

Disclaimer

The information in this instruction book is presented in good faith. However, no warranty is given, nor
results guaranteed, nor is freedom from any patent to be inferred. Since we have no control over the
use of information contained in this book, the publisher and the author disclaim liability for untoward results.

10 9 8 7 6 5 4

Acknowledgements

There have been many wonderful friends and family who have loved and supported me during the writing of this, my third book. I am not sure that I had the courage on my own to see this book to fruition without their faith in me. In particular, my husband Peter, my two children, Cara and Guy, and especially my dear friend Jenny, who is always by my side giving me constant and gentle encouragement.

To Lea-Anne and Coralie, thank you for your valuable contributions.

And to Tracy Bradbury and Richard Galbraith, thank you both for your gifts of the two wonderful bear designs.

Profile

Pamela Gurney has had a long love of needlework and handicraft beginning when she was a very young girl. She became enthralled with punchneedle embroidery in the early 1990s and since then her interest has grown to a passion. Pamela is currently the leading proponent of this form of needle art. Since 1997 she has written three books of which this is the third. She has also produced a high-quality video and invented her own Dancing Ribbon Needle for silk-ribbon punch embroidery. She has her own business, Dancing Needle Designs, which provides all requirements for the punchneedle beginner and enthusiast.

Pamela works from her home-based studio in the Australian bush close to Melbourne. She conducts classes and is represented at needlecraft shows all around Australia and has introduced thousands of Australians to the enjoyment of punchneedle embroidery. She also has a growing list of overseas clients, particularly in the USA, South-East Asia and Europe, and aims to travel widely overseas teaching and encouraging people with their punchneedle embroidery. This book is written for the wider audience and seeks to encourage new and more experienced embroiderers to enjoy the dimensional, colourful and exciting pieces that can be created by embroidering with punchneedles.

Contents

PROJECTS

Introduction

When I was a little girl I watched my mother, every evening after the completion of her never-ending chores (we were a family of eleven, on a sheep and wheat farm in Western Australia), remove her apron, sit down for probably the first time all day, and take up her crochet hook. She finally relaxed and became engrossed in her needlework. I pondered on this for years. I now know that when women take time to sit and immerse themselves in their craft work they go to a 'special' place within.

At the time of writing this, my third book, the world is witnessing turbulent times and it does well to retreat into a calm and special place while we work our embroidery—my needles continue to dance, and I have been sharing this amazing dance with thousands of people around the world. It is my wish that in these climactic times I can continue to touch thousands more with my beloved Dancing Needle Embroidery (punchneedle embroidery). It is so meditative and relaxing to sit with this gentle needle art. Like my mother, I hope that you can find that 'special' place while you are quietly embroidering with your Dancing Needles.

It is also my hope that your beautiful punchneedle embroideries will be loved and cared for so that future generations will enjoy them.

May your needles dance forever.

PAMELA

1. What is punchneedle embroidery?

Punchneedle embroidery, worked with a special tool, stands alone in its ability to create the most textural of all embroideries. Depending on the size of the punchneedle, this technique uses a vast array of threads and ribbons which can add life, colour, texture and richness to embroideries. The colours, types, thickness and textures of the myriad of threads to be found are exciting. All of these factors bring the 'shimmer' phenomenon into an embroidery. So long as a thread can be easily threaded and will flow smoothly through the eye of the punchneedle, it can be used. From my experience and years of experimentation almost any thread available can be used if it passes this test.

Unlike traditional embroidery, punchneedle embroidery requires a design to be printed or traced onto the back of the fabric to be embroidered. With a threaded punchneedle, the embroiderer makes a small running stitch on the back of the fabric following the traced design. To form this running stitch and to keep the stitch in place, the needle is 'punched' through to the front of the fabric where a loop of thread is formed. It is the loop on the front that outlines or fills in the embroidery.

This technique creates a beautiful textured finish. The loops can be short, long, trimmed, fringed or shaped to give a wide range of textural effects to enhance a design.

There are inspirations for patterns and designs all around us. Fabrics, wrapping paper, magazines, cards, dinnerware and children's books are just a few areas from where inspiration can be obtained. Patterns are also available from many embroidery designers.

If copying someone else's design keep in mind the issue of copyright and take this into consideration. For your own peace of mind and to protect artists, try to understand copyright issues. A good place to start is www.copyright.org.au. Of course, you can always draw your own designs and enjoy working them perhaps even more.

I have developed the designs for this book to both give enjoyment and provide a challenge for the embroiderer. Some of the designs have been expressly chosen to include a lesson within them. For example, the miniature carpet design is a lesson on how you can achieve an original design by using a design sourced from elsewhere. It takes you through a process of how to easily draw your very own design.

There are important hints and tips scattered in and about all of the projects. I suggest that you read through the project instructions and hints before you start working. This will provide an overall understanding of the techniques involved and if you need to, you can refer back to the relevant technique elsewhere in the book to clarify an issue before you start work.

The English embroider, designer and author Richard Box says, 'Do not dislike what you do—see your work through to completion.' This is so right with the technique of punchneedle embroidery. When only one or two rows of loops are looked at on the front of a piece, it is so easy to say, 'Oh, it looks terrible.' (I hear this constantly in my classes.) But when the piece is near completion or is entirely finished people are thrilled with how good their work looks. Please keep going to see your embroidery through to the end. I respond to people in my class who make this comment with: 'There is never a mistake, always a result. It might not be the one you want but you will have a beautiful embroidery at the end if you just keep going and finish the piece.'

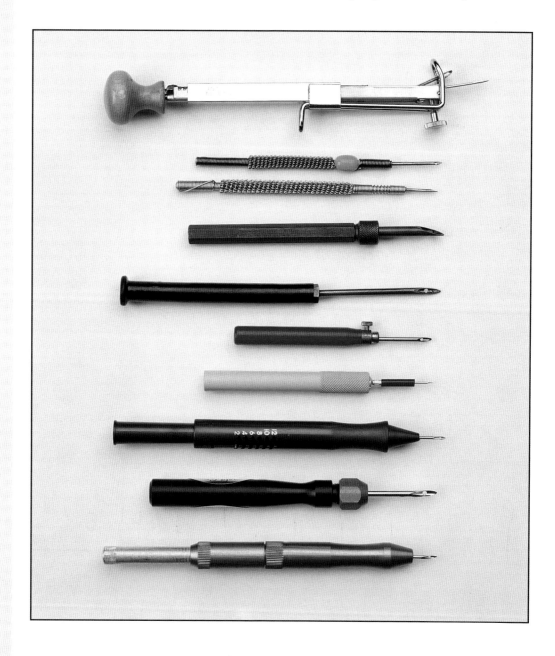

A variety of punchneedles in my collection

Punchneedles

There are many varieties of punchneedles available and they all work on the same basic principle.

Generally a punchneedle will have a handle and a needle tip. The handle may be made of brass, plastic, wood or bakelite with the needle tips made from stainless steel, surgical steel, brass or other types of metal. The handle and needle are hollow allowing the passage of a thread through them. The needle tip has a bevelled (slanted) side and a straight side. The eye of the punchneedle is a hole on the straight side of the needle. With some experimentation and adaptation, most types of punchneedles can be used to make interesting pieces of embroidery.

Regardless of the type you use, the final result of a running stitch on the back forming a loop on the front will be achieved. The end effect can range from quite primitive to highly artistic depending on the tool and the execution of the stitch. The result achieved to some extent depends upon the implement's capabilities and some punchneedles will be able to do more or less than others. Of course, the skill and practice of the embroiderer is a consideration.

Having different sized punchneedles will be an advantage. Some punchneedles are so fine as to only allow very fine thread to be threaded through them. Others are larger, and some can take interchangeable needle tips which allow the use of fine threads, thicker thread, wool and ribbons. You will get the most from your punchneedles if you give time to experiment and practice.

It is a good idea to initially work on a practice piece of embroidery. Use this to check the type and thickness of thread that can be worked through the needle and the type of fabric that the punchneedle is most compatible with (see Threads, page 63; Fabrics, page 50).

Whatever punchneedle you have I am sure that my designs will work well after you have a little play, and I hope that my ideas are a source of inspiration for you.

Pile depth

Each type of punchneedle has its own unique way of altering the length of the needle tip and thus the length of the loop formed on the front of the fabric—the pile depth. The needle tip can be punched through the fabric only as far as the handle of the punchneedle or to the end of a gauge placed on a needle. The gauge or other methods used with various punchneedles sets the depth to which the needle can be inserted into the fabric and gives evenness to the loops created.

Some punchneedles require a small piece of plastic tube being slipped over the needle tip to restrict how far the needle will go into the fabric. This alters the pile depth or loop size. For these punchneedles, one measures from the eye of the needle and then cuts the plastic tube the appropriate length to give the length of pile depth required for a particular project.

Other punchneedles have built-in mechanisms which very easily alter the length of the needle. With some punchneedles, the needle holder within the casing of the handle is twisted up and down resulting in a longer or shorter

TIP

I have worked most of the designs in this book using the Ultra-Punch needle. The Magical Miniature Carpet was worked with a very fine needle, and A Promise of Summer with the Dancing Ribbon needle. It is important that you first experiment with your own punchneedles as your needle might work a little finer or larger than my needle. You may need to slightly alter the size of a pattern or use shorter loops to accommodate your punchneedle.

needle tip. Yet another type of punchneedle has a spring and gauge which simply allows the needle holder in the handle casing to be pushed up and down and locked into different settings. This needle is particularly easy to use and to adjust the pile depth with the minimum of fuss and time.

For punchneedles using plastic tubing, the plastic is either purchased with the punchneedle or alternatively can be made from the insulating plastic surrounding narrow-gauge electrical wire after removing the wire. If the plastic is initially too tight to slip onto the needle, soak it in warm water to soften it. It may be too loose, in which case thread a piece of thread through the tube to give a tighter fit when placed onto the needle.

The pile depth is measured from the eye of the needle to the end of the plastic tube being used as the gauge, or to the bottom of the handle in some types of punchneedles.

The length of the loop formed on the front of the fabric is half the measurement for the pile depth. A pile depth of

25 mm (1 in) will give a loop of 12 mm (½ in). Some of the length of the loop will be taken up by the thickness of the fabric. This needs to be considered if using a thick, fluffy woollen blanket fabric for example.

To make a very short loop, shorter than the shortest needle setting when using a gauge-controlled needle, cut a piece of plastic tubing to shorten the length of the needle to 6 mm (¼ in). If the plastic tube is cut too long it will result in a loop that is too short and which will not stay in the fabric. If this happens, shorten the length of the plastic by a millimetre or two and try again.

Some needle tips have their length measured in millimetres, others by numbers and yet others by letters of the alphabet. In this book all needle tip measurements are given numerically, with the lowest number being the shortest needle length. The guide below is applicable for conversion for various types of punchneedles to the projects in this book.

Ruler

Conversion chart

Setting	Needle length (mm)	Needle length (inches)
No 1	9–10 mm	⅜ inch
No 2	11–12 mm	approx. ½ inch
No 3	12–13 mm	½ inch
No 4	14 mm	⅝ inch
No 5	15 mm	a little over ⅝ inch
No 6	17 mm	approx. ¾ inch
No 7	18 mm	¾ inch
No 8	20 mm	a little over ¾ inch
No 9	21 mm	⅞ inch
No 10	23 mm	a little over ⅞ inch
No 11	25 mm	1 inch
No 12	26–27 mm	1 ⅛ inch

The conversion chart is approximate only, as needle tip lengths can vary. The projects in this book may be successfully worked with an allowance of needle tip length of 1–2 mm.

The Dancing Ribbon needle

This is a punchneedle designed to embroider with 7–13 mm (approximately ¼–½ in) silk ribbon. The results achieved with the Dancing Ribbon needle are exquisite. The Dancing Ribbon needle is a punchneedle, and the way one uses it is only a little different to the smaller types of punchneedle. In common with other punchneedle embroidery the design is marked on the back of the fabric and the project worked from there. After drawing the design and placing the fabric very taut in the hoop, the needle tip of your Dancing Ribbon needle is placed at the point of insertion and guided through the fabric with a gentle twisting action. This allows the tip to delicately find its way between the fibres of the fabric without causing much damage. More precise instructions for its use appear in A Promise of Summer.

Threaders

A punchneedle cannot be threaded without an appropriate threader, often a specially adapted fine wire with a looped end. All punchneedles are threaded in a similar manner. Threaders have two loops, the larger of which the thread is passed through, and then the thread is

A threader with a paper or plastic tag

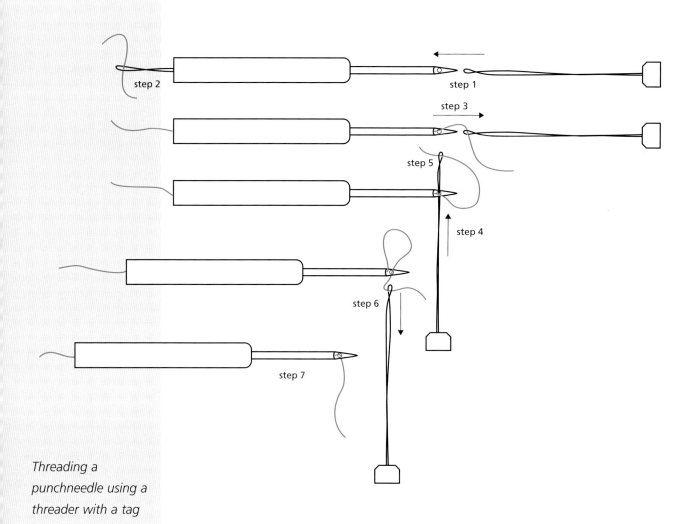

Threading a punchneedle using a threader with a tag

gently pulled through the smaller loop to hold it in place while the thread is being pulled through the hollow of the needle. See Threading a Punchneedle below for more specific instructions, and read the instructions which come with your set of punchneedles.

Threading a punchneedle is a two-step process. You have to thread the bore of the needle and then thread the eye of the needle.

Step 1. The threader is first inserted from the sharp end of the needle tip, up through the hollow bore of the needle and handle until the looped end of the threader protrudes from the handle.

Step 2. Pass the thread through the loops and pull it into the small twisted loop at the end of the threader. This holds the thread securely while it is pulled back through the bore of the needle.

Step 3. Pull the threader by the tag all the way back through the handle and needle until the threader and thread are clear of the needle tip. Unthread the thread from the threader. You have now threaded the bore of the needle, but you still need to thread the eye of the needle.

Step 4. Insert the looped end of the threader from the straight side (eye

16

side) of the needle through the eye of the needle.

Step 5. Thread the thread back through the loops of the threader, pull the thread up into the twist and then:

Step 6. Draw the thread back through the eye of the needle.

Step 7. Remove the thread from the threader and carefully put the threader and the threaded punchneedle away until you are ready to commence embroidering.

Care and safety

The precise machining of punchneedles means they need to be carefully looked after. The tips must be prevented from becoming damaged or burred from being dropped or stabbed into harsh objects. Some punchneedles have a spring-loaded action which enables the needle tip to be retracted and housed safely. Others come with plastic sheaths in which the needle tip is placed when not in use.

It is very important that punchneedles be kept out of reach of toddlers and that children use them only under close supervision. Be careful of your own fingers (and your thighs if you have the habit of working on your lap). These are rather long sharp implements which can cause a nasty scratch or prick. Work safely.

Threaders are quite fragile and easily broken, therefore they require gentle handling. Threaders are an integral part of the threading process and, as they can be easily lost, find a container to store them safely in.

A gentle word of caution—refrain from putting a threader in your mouth as it can readily pinch or cut your tongue.

TIP

It is possible to thread some of the large punchneedles in one movement (such as the large Ultra-Punch needle and Dancing Ribbon needle). Push the threader through the eye of the needle, bend the tip of the threader slightly and guide it into the bore of the needle. Push the threader all the way through the bore and handle until it shows. Take the thread through the twisted loop of the threader and then pull the threader back through the bore and the needle in one motion. (See Threading under A Promise of Summer.)

2 Punchneedle embroidery techniques

Allow yourself time to practice and time to get to know the gentle needle art of punchneedle embroidery. The more skills you learn the more exciting the dance with your punchneedles becomes.

Setting up

Assemble the fabric very tightly in the hoop. Have the nut on the hoop at the very top (12 o'clock) and facing to the right if you are right-handed (to the left for left-handed embroiderers). This means that the nut is up and out of the way which will prevent the working thread from getting caught around it.

Straighten the design in the hoop so that it is not distorted from the tight stretching.

Thread the punchneedle as described on page 16. Check the flow of the thread by pulling it gently to and fro through the needle. If it is too tight or too loose, either change the needle size or change the thread.

Look at the needle tip. There is a bevelled edge, that is, the edge cut on a slant, and a straight edge with the eye.

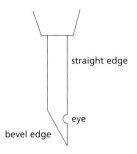

straight edge

eye

bevel edge

Punchneedle tip (greatly enlarged)

Direction of work

My personal choice for stitching is almost always to work towards myself. I constantly turn the hoop when embroidering so that the needle is always travelling toward me. As I am right handed I have the bevelled edge of the needle facing to the left while I stitch and the eye of the needle to the right. For left-handed people turn the bevel to the right and the eye to the left.

The way you choose to work with the needle is a personal thing and may differ to my preference. Work in whatever manner is most comfortable, so long as the formed loops meet your requirements, give adequate coverage on the front of the fabric, and look good.

Sit at a table. Hold the hoop, resting the edge closest to you on the table and the far side of the hoop high enough above the table so as not to punch into the tabletop and thereby damage the tip of the needle.

How to make the stitch

You will generally be working from the back of the fabric to the front, so the wrong side of the fabric needs to be uppermost in the hoop. It is far easier to stitch on the flat, tight face of the fabric in the hoop than to work into the concavity of the hoop.

Hold the punchneedle like a pen. Rest the side of your hand and your little finger on the stretched fabric in the hoop. It is best that you are not holding the hoop underneath with the little finger of your stitching hand. Your hand needs to be free to move unrestricted over the fabric.

Hold the punchneedle at a little less than right angles to the fabric (that is, slightly off the vertical).

There is no set place to start stitching. Obviously if an outline is to be worked you will start at a logical place or where on a design the instructions suggest that you start.

Work safely. Be sure to keep your fingers away from the underside of the fabric where they might get pricked.

With your needle on the setting appropriate for the pattern, punch through the fabric as far as the needle can be punched. Every stitch is punched to the full depth of either the plastic on the needle tip or, if needle length (pile depth) is set by a gauge, to the hilt of the needle. Each stitch punched fully to this depth gives uniformity to the length of the loops formed.

There is no knotting or oversewing to begin or end the stitching. You can, however, work a couple of backstitches to start and finish if you wish. Work two stitches backwards, and then stitch forward immediately on top of these. This assists in holding the beginning and ending stitches in place.

A tag of thread will be left on the back at the point of entry of the needle. This needs to be only about 6–10 mm (¼–½ inch) long, depending on the thread being used. The ends of some fine

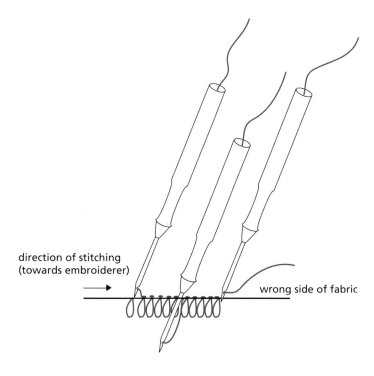

direction of stitching
(towards embroiderer)

wrong side of fabric

This shows the method of stitching from the side view for ease of illustration. Position the needle as shown with the bevel (angle) of the needle tip facing to the left for right-handed embroiderers (to the right if left-handed).

or slippery threads may have a tendency to find their way to the front of the fabric. If that is the case, leave a longer tag and trim later.

Withdraw the punchneedle a little and turn it in your fingers until you can see the start of the bevel. Withdraw the needle until the tip barely clears the surface of the fabric. Skim the needle along the surface for a very short distance and punch it into the fabric again. Listen to the dragging sound this makes for the first dozen or so stitches until the action becomes natural. The motion for working becomes a lift-slide-punch, lift-slide-punch action. Avoid lifting the needle tip

clear away from the fabric as this can pull the loops you have just punched out of the fabric.

An indicator of how far apart the straight stitches made on the back of the fabric need to be is the width of the needle being used. It takes only a short time before you are aware of how long the stitches need to be and how close to work the rows.

Turn your work over to check your progress. If your stitches are close enough together on the back they will make an unbroken row of loops on the front. If there are gaps in the line of the loops, this indicates that you need to make your stitches a bit closer together. When a second row of stitches is made close to the first row, the loops of that row will fill up any small spaces of the previous row on the front of the fabric.

Be sure that the thread is flowing freely through the needle and is not knotted or caught around anything.

During the stitching process try to avoid punching into the previous row of stitches—if this happens, already formed loops can be pushed longer than desired. Whenever possible, it is important to have the needle angled away from the row of stitches just worked. A right-handed embroiderer will work with the straight edge of the needle on the left side of the previous row of stitches (left-handed embroiderers will work opposite to this).

If a right handed embroiderer works on the right side of the previous row with the needle angled towards the left, it is easy for the loops of the previous row to be punched through, and also to be pushed longer than the desired length. In this situation the front loops may look scruffy and time and patience will be needed to tidy them up. When this occurs and longer loops form on the front, gently pull the loop down to the desired length with a fine crochet hook from the back, with the embroidery tight in the hoop.

There will be a few instances when it is necessary to work from the 'wrong' side of a previous row. Just work slowly and carefully in these situations and, if necessary, tidy up as described above.

It is quite acceptable to switch from one area of colour on the design to another of the same colour without cutting the thread. Hold the thread in place at the point of exit, pull the punchneedle along the thread, start in the new spot and when a few stitches have been punched, trim the looped thread between the areas. Keep the back of your work free from loops and long ends as these can easily get caught and pull out previously worked loops.

Check the loop spacing on the front of the work. The distance between the stitches is short and the distance between the rows is barely a needle width. When the finished piece is held up to the light, ideally there will be no gaps or unworked areas of fabric to be seen. If there are gaps, simply fill in with a few more stitches.

You need to reach a happy medium. If the stitching and rows are worked too closely the piece will curl when removed from the hoop, if not close enough, the coverage on the front will be patchy.

Allow the thread to flow all the way through the needle when a length of thread is finished. Sometimes the ends of the thread finish up on the front of the work and need to be carefully pulled through to the back with the crochet hook.

The fabric always needs to be very tight in the hoop. If it becomes slightly slack, use gentle pressure with your fingers to push up from under the hoop or down from the top of the fabric with your thumb to create more tension. While embroidering, regularly tighten the fabric and retighten the hoop nut as necessary. Read the section on Hoop Techniques for further ideas.

Cutting threads

To cut the thread upon completion of a section of stitching, hold it in place with your index finger at the point of exit. Slide the needle some way along the thread, then punch the needle into the fabric for safekeeping and to prevent it rolling. Cut the thread leaving a short tag. The last loops made may be pulled out if the thread is not held firmly.

If there are any thread tags or long loops on the front of the embroidery, pull them to the back of the fabric before trimming them. A crochet hook is helpful for this. You can cut threads on the front of the embroidery, but be aware that some threads change colour dramatically when cut and can show noticeably as a very different colour or look like a dirty mark. This is a technique that can be used to great advantage where a deeper shade of a colour will add effect to a design (see figure 20, Stitch Glossary).

Finishing off

On the completion of a project you need to use your own judgement on the appearance of the work from the front. The front may require tidying up of long loops and end tags or more loops may need to be

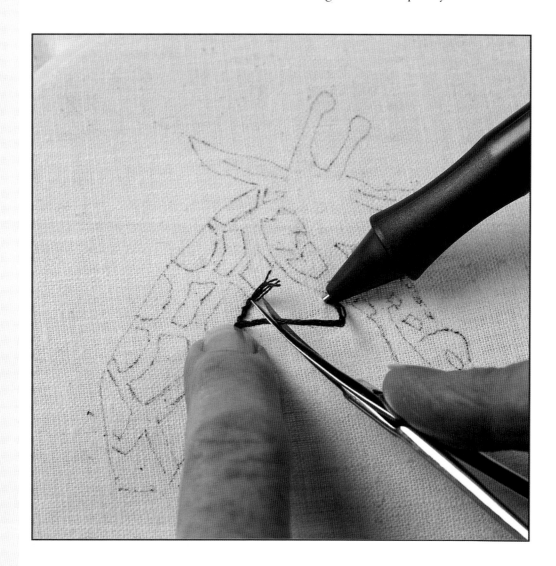

Cutting the ends of the thread on the back of the work

embroidered to fill in a sparse area.

Check your work thoroughly before removing it from the hoop. Remember, as Richard Box says: 'Good finishing is the perfect complement to good embroidery and a piece of work can be made or marred in the final stages.' Richard is a talented English embroiderer, designer and author. His books *Colour and Design for Embroidery* and *Drawing and Design for Embroidery* (Batsford) are a great resource for all embroiderers.

Troubleshooting

'Oh, dear! Nothing's happening!' This is a cry I hear frequently. There are a number of things to look out for if you are experiencing 'nothing happening'.

◆ It is a two-part process to thread the needle. Firstly, check that the thread is passed through the bore of the punchneedle, secondly, that it is threaded through the eye of the needle.

◆ Check that the thread is flowing freely. The thread flows from the end of the punchneedle over your wrist so your arm is not resting on the thread. Take care that the thread is not wrapped around your fingers or being held alongside the needle. It is easy for the thread to get caught on something preventing it from flowing freely. If the thread is not flowing, a loop is unable to form.

◆ During the punching process, if the needle is lifted clear of the fabric and not closely skimmed across the surface, the loops previously made will be pulled out of the fabric.

◆ There are times when a knot or clump of thread is pulled into the handle. When all of the above have been checked, it may be necessary to cut the thread, and take the punchneedle apart to see if something is amiss inside the punchneedle itself. Often a thread from a frayed edge of the fabric (it is a good idea to overlock or tape any frayed edges), or another piece of thread can attach to the thread being used. When these all pass through the needle they can clog up the bore.

◆ If the needle tip is not long enough then a sufficiently long loop is not formed to stay in the fabric. When loops are too short they cannot stay in place.

◆ When things just aren't progressing, the most important issue is whether the fabric is tight enough in the hoop (see Hoop Techniques, page 55). When the entire list above has been worked through, check the fabric in the hoop. With loose, baggy fabric in the hoop, loops in punchneedle embroidery are unable to form properly.

◆ When the incorrect thread thickness has been chosen for a particular size needle, either the thread is too thick to flow through the needle, or it is too fine, when it simply runs through the needle too quickly.

◆ The needle tip needs to be travelling forward. If inadvertently you are stitching backwards it is easy to punch the needle through the thread, cutting and shredding it.

- The stitches on the back are usually spaced about a needle-width apart. Where a short needle length is set and the running stitches on the back are spaced too far apart, some of the loop length will be taken up on the back of the work as a straight stitch and the loops will not be long enough to stay in place.

- Where a lot of unpicking has been done, the fibres of the fabric can become fragile, and even severely damaged. It is the weave of the fabric which holds the loops in place. When the weave is damaged, the loops cannot possibly be held in place. Try some iron-on woven interfacing behind the damaged fabric to overcome this—see below.

Repairing a hole

Sometimes you wonder how it happens! But holes can be made in the fabric being embroidered. Where a lot of unpicking has taken place the fabric can be damaged. Silly as it sounds, I have actually cut a hole in the fabric of an almost completed embroidery. If a large punchneedle has been chosen for a fine fabric, the needle can easily cut the fibres of the weave.

There are a few ways to 'fix a hole':

- The damaged area can be 'darned'. Stitch in replacement warp and weft fibres with an ordinary sewing needle.

- Remove the fabric from the hoop. Take a small piece of iron-on woven interfacing and, with the tip of a heated iron, press the piece in place.

- If iron-on woven interfacing is not available, simply lightly glue a piece of woven fabric into place. Leave to dry before doing any further punching.

- Hold a piece of woven fabric over the damaged area and gently punch some loops through this. Trim the fabric when the area has been repaired.

- Stitching with a sewing needle threaded with a matching colour, make some loops the same height. You will need something to anchor the loops on, so lay a pin across the hole on the back and work over it. Glue over the back of the loops and before the glue is completely dry, remove the pin.

Overview

Let's review what we've covered so far. To work this gentle needle art, a design is traced onto the back of the fabric to be embroidered. The fabric is then placed into a special lip-lock hoop where it is pulled very tight, thus opening up the weave. A beautiful little running stitch is worked on the back which in turn forms a loop on the front. The loop can be varied in length to create added depth. The whole process culminates in a unique, richly textured and highly dimensional embroidery.

Note, however, that when you are working traditional, that is, 'normal', punchneedle embroidery, you need to refrain from cutting any long loops that sit up higher than any others on the front of the work. The reason for this is that some threads change colour dramatically when cut, thus leaving dark marks which show up noticeably on the finished work. This quality can, however, be used to great advantage where a deeper shade of a colour will add effect to a design. Cutting loops very low can change the look of the embroidery from a textured pile appearance to a wonderful rich plush velvet look. For some wonderful examples, see figure 20, Stitch Glossary.

I hear this question repeatedly: 'If I pull that, will it all come out?'

Let me explain. 'That' means the beginning or ending tag of thread on the back of the work. The answer, simply, is yes. Pull the tag of thread while the fabric is in the hoop and yes, some loops can be pulled out because the weave of the fabric has been stretched wide open. However, it is very difficult to pull out the loops from the front of the piece even when in the hoop. When the fabric is removed from the hoop it is quite a different story—the stitches on the back, and the loops on the front, are equally secure and quite difficult to accidentally pull out. The weave of the fabric relaxes around the formed loops.

There are a number of principles that need to be understood. Traditionally, punchneedle embroidery was designed to be worked with the stitches close together and thus the loops on the front of the embroidery are very close together. When worked like this it is extremely difficult for 'it all to come out'. The stitches are close together, the loops get caught up with each other, the filaments of the spun and twisted threads become intermeshed and one will have

the dickens of a job to pull the embroidery undone. The loop when punched through the fabric also twists on itself a little and opens out, becoming bigger than the hole made for the passage of the needle. Added to this, when the embroidery is removed from the hoop the fabric, which was stretched taut, relaxes and the weave clutches onto the threads. Further to this, if you wash the completed piece the threads and fabric shrink a little and some threads will matt as well. All of these factors collectively explain why a completed piece of punchneedle embroidery can not readily be pulled out.

Remember the importance of having the fabric very tight in the hoop where the weave is stretched open, allowing the needle to easily penetrate the fabric without damaging the fibres. During the process of the embroidery there is very little holding the last stitches punched, and that is why when the tag is pulled some stitches can be undone from the back. Remember, you can work a couple of backstitches for added security.

The principles above need to be understood for one to realise the difference between this method of embroidery and traditional hand embroidery, in which stitches are worked up and over the weave of the fabric to be held in place.

When punchneedle embroidery is worked in the normal manner, that is, with the punched loops very close together, a completed piece will wash and wash and have a very long life to become an heirloom.

There are many other methods of

TIP

When working a floral design, from time to time place the piece in front of a mirror so you can see it in reverse. This is a great way to check the balance of a design. Doing this makes it easy to see if the floral arrangement is lopsided and where more loops might be necessary.

stitching within the spectrum of punchneedle embroidery, aside from punching loops very close together, and some of these will not stand up to day-to-day use or washing. Those pieces which are embellished with surface stitches, such as reverse punchneedle embroidery (see Stitch Glossary), will need to be framed or have a smear of glue over the back of the stitching to hold the stitches in place.

The use of glue

Traditionally punchneedle embroidery was designed to be worked with the loops very close together and with short loops close to the fabric. When worked in this manner, the embroidery will hold in place very securely. It can generally be safely washed and in fact seems to improve with washing. (See also under Appliqué, page 59.) This is certainly so with some of my appliquéd embroidery on handtowels. When appliquéd on knitted sweatshirt fabric the embroidery will far outlast the garment itself, even after much washing.

Over the years I have been having a merry dance with my punchneedles and I have discovered and developed many new decorative stitches, which can be seen in the Stitch Glossary. These stitches generally rely for their effect on being worked on the front of the embroidery, mostly with only one row of decorative stitching standing alone. One row of punchneedle embroidery cannot be expected to stay in place through wear and tear and washing. This was never the intention for the technique of decorative

punchneedle embroidery and this is when I use a little glue to help hold the stitches permanently in place. However, where these decorative stitches are used on a piece of embroidery for framing, I do not glue them. I consider that the framed piece is special and I want it to be framed as conservatively as possible. Anyway, as the framed piece will not be handled or need washing, the stitches will not be at risk of being accidentally pulled out.

There will, however, be times when surface stitches are used on pieces of punchneedle embroidery used for interior decoration, for example cushions, bedspreads or table runners. In these instances it is best that where a single row of decorative surface stitching is embroidered that a light smear of good quality craft glue is applied to the loops on the back. The decorative stitches when lightly glued become more stable and are unlikely to be accidentally pulled out.

Working with silk ribbon

Note These instructions refer to working silk ribbons with the larger sizes of punchneedle, like the large Ultra-Punch needle. Instructions for working silk ribbons with the Dancing Ribbon needle are included in the project A Promise of Summer, the only project in this book that uses the Dancing Ribbon needle.

Working with silk ribbon is slightly different.

A large needle tip threaded with wide silk ribbon can easily damage the fibres of the fabric when punched through the fabric. Thus, the motion is to gently twist the needle tip carefully through the weave and to push the needle tip down as far as it can go. Avoid the punch-punch-punch motion when using silk ribbons. Usually with punchneedle embroidery there is no knotting to commence the stitching.

Silk ribbon is slippery and can very quickly and frustratingly become unthreaded from the punchneedle. Also, the beginning tag of the silk ribbon frequently finds its way through to the front of the fabric. Therefore, I suggest that when the needle is threaded, a small knot be tied on the end of the ribbon protruding from the needle tip. The knot will keep the needle threaded and will stop the beginning tag from working its way through to the front of the fabric.

You can also leave a length sufficient to tie a knot in the end tag of the ribbon when you have finished working, but this can waste expensive ribbon. I feel that a knot at the beginning is sufficient, as it at least prevents some of the ends from escaping through to the front.

You can also smear a little (just a little) glue onto the ends of the ribbon at the completion of each flower to help keep them in place.

If an end of ribbon finds its way through to the front of the fabric, use a small crochet hook to carefully grasp it and pull it through again to the back.

It is important that any long loops of silk ribbon already created are held out of the way of other loops being made. This is to prevent the punchneedle piercing them, which makes them look tatty. It also prevents the long loops becoming intermingled or embroidered together, which precludes the petals from opening fully. While holding long loops out of the way on the front of the fabric, embroider slowly, working safely and gently to prevent stabbing your fingers.

When each area or flower is completed, check on the front that the long loops are not caught in other loops. If they are, gently release them with your fingers.

3 Stitch glossary

'The needle must dance and sing.'

Punchneedle embroidery is a fascinating needle art. It is so versatile and there are many ways that the one basic, simple stitch of this technique can be employed to create an almost never-ending series of effects rich in texture and using a huge range of threads.

The embroidery samples in this book illustrate some of the different stitch variations which can be made with the punchneedle. Like everything, taking the time to practice is of the essence. Some people consider punchneedle embroidery as being easy and fast. Certainly this is the case when there is little variation in the loop size. The Handstand Clown is an example of this type of project. Terrific use of colour and an interesting design, but largely one loop size which means the project is rather more quickly finished than some other projects that have a far greater textural variety. A more detailed project with stitch variety and artistic interpretation, such as the Circle Upon a Circle, requires more time and patience to execute. Remember though, punchneedle embroidery is nearly always considerably faster than traditional embroidery. Circle Upon a Circle emulates traditional hand embroidery stitches with a spectacularly delightful result.

Traditional punchneedle embroidery

Traditional punchneedle embroidery, the basis of all punchneedle embroidery, or what I refer to as 'normal punchneedle embroidery', is small, straight running stitches punched from the back of the fabric which form loops on the front. The design being used is traced onto the back of the fabric and the embroidery is worked from the back of the fabric. There is no knotting or tying of the starting and finishing thread ends in this technique. You can, however, work a couple of backstitches to start and finish. Work two stitches backwards, and then stitch forward immediately on top of these. This assists in holding the first and last stitches in place. A variety of textures can then be created by altering between short loops and long loops. The long loops can be cut, trimmed, fringed or sculpted or merely left as large, full loops. The result is always spectacular.

Figure 1
Sample a The top sample and the stitching on the left shows normal punchneedle embroidery viewed from the back. Punching from the back creates a small running stitch. Sample a has been worked with three strands of embroidery cotton. When more or fewer strands of thread, or different threads, are used, the

appearance of the stitches alters. The tag which is normally left on the back has been cut very short for the purposes of photography and can normally be left a bit longer.

Sample b The bottom sample and the stitches on the right show the loops which are formed on the front.

Figure 2

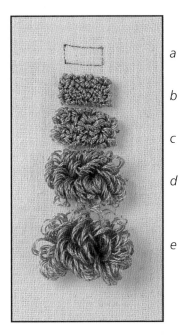

The box drawn on the fabric is the same sized box that all of the samples have been worked in. The samples have all been worked in three strands of embroidery cotton with varying length of loops from No 1 to No 12 (see Pile Depth, page 13).

By increasing the length of the needle and then punching through the fabric to the hilt of the needle with each stitch, larger loops are created on the front of the fabric. The larger the loops on the front of the fabric, the more area occupied by the stitches! Figure 2, sample e, indicates the importance of remembering how much more fabric area outside of the drawn square is taken up by the embroidery, as the loops made on the front are longer.

Reverse punchneedle embroidery

This is seen in figure 7, sample a, on page 35.

As explained above, in traditional punchneedle embroidery a small running stitch is the basis of punchneedle embroidery. When this running stitch is worked from the front of the fabric an interesting surface stitch is created. When embroidered with a punchneedle on the front of the fabric this running stitch alters the whole concept of punchneedle embroidery. I call this 'reverse punchneedle embroidery', and by using it in your punchneedle embroidery a host of different surface stitches can be executed which offers a new and exciting entrée into the wonderland of punchneedle embroidery.

As reverse punchneedle embroidery is embroidered on the front of the fabric it is necessary to trace that part of the design onto the front of the fabric. Trace a very fine and light line with either a well-sharpened lead pencil or a water-erasable pen. The finished embroidery normally covers over the traced line. A line made with a water-erasable pen will fade in a few hours, or you can wipe away any line marking that shows with a slightly damp cloth.

To get the perfect reverse stitch it is necessary to have the fabric as taut as possible in the hoop and to practice. Having the fabric drum-tight in the hoop is really important for punchneedle embroidery. How to achieve this is explained under Hoop Techniques, page 55. Ideally, for complete control and to achieve perfect stitches it is best if reverse punchneedle embroidery is done with the design facing uppermost in the hoop. Sure, you can work within the concavity of the hoop but it is not so easy or pleasant.

The beginning and ending threads of reverse punchneedle embroidery need to be pulled through to the back of the piece being worked. To do this simply punch the needle into the front of the fabric. Then turn the hoop over with the needle still in situ, and either with your fingers or a fine pair of pointy tweezers, pull the thread emerging from the fabric through to the back. This is the starting tag of the thread. To shorten this tag, take the thread where it enters the handle of the punchneedle and withdraw the thread until only a short tag remains. This is all a bit of a juggling act, but with practice it becomes second nature. Okay! Complete the area to be stitched.

Now, how to get the finishing end through to the back? Leave the punchneedle in the fabric. Turn the hoop over and with your fingers or tweezers, take the thread emerging from the eye of the needle and pull it to a sufficient length to cut it. At this time, if you pull the thread from the base of the fabric, you will undo some of your beautiful stitches. Cut the thread. Withdraw the punchneedle from the fabric, leaving the end tag on the back. As you withdraw the punchneedle, hold the last stitch made in place.

After removing the needle there may well be a small entry hole left in the fabric. From the back and using your index finger scratch the fibres of the weave to close them around the thread and the hole magically disappears!

Reverse punchneedle embroidery leaves loops on the back of the fabric. When a completed piece of embroidery worked with a lot of reverse stitching is stretched for framing the loops may cause a bulge which looks a little unsightly. This can be easily overcome by placing wadding or pellon under the embroidery on completion. The loops nestle into the soft padding, which prevents a bulge appearing when the piece is mounted for framing.

Figure 3

This shows the different appearances or finishes which can be achieved with reverse punchneedle embroidery.

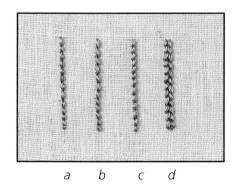

a   b   c   d

Sample a Shows how the stitch looks when worked with the bevelled edge of the needle directly forward. The running stitch appears to be straight.

Sample b Shows the beautiful effect to the running stitch when the bevelled edge of the needle is facing to the left for right-handed embroiderers (or facing to the right for left-handed embroiderers) and stitching forward. This looks just like the most perfect stem stitch made with traditional hand embroidery.

Sample c The bevelled edge is facing the left; however, the stitch is worked backwards. The difference in the look of the stitch is subtle but it is more raised. Thicker threads give it a bolder finish.

Sample d A row of stitching is worked forward, with a second row worked backwards close to it on the left, giving a lovely chain/rope effect.

Counting stitches

In many of my designs I suggest how many stitches to make. This refers to the straight running stitch formed either on the front or back of the embroidery.

Punch the needle into the fabric and withdraw it. This of course leaves a loop on the other side. This is not counted as a stitch. Punch the needle into the fabric again, and count the first straight stitch linking the two loops created on the front as stitch number 1.

Continue punching and counting the stitches until the required number has been worked.

Figure 4 is an exaggerated example of this for ease of viewing. There are 10 counted stitches which will produce 11 loops.

The number of stitches that I suggest is a guide only, as we all work differently. You may find that more or less stitches are needed for the required area of embroidery.

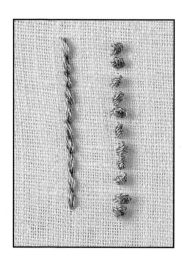

Working in a circle

Once you have mastered working in a circle your punchneedle embroidery will never be the same. It opens up a vast new breadth to the traditional punchneedle embroidery known by thousands of people.

In the section Direction of Work on page 18 I mention that I always stitch with the punchneedle travelling towards me (directly forward). I turn my hoop constantly so that this is achieved. To work a circle it is a constant movement of punching a few stitches, turning the hoop, punching and turning, punching and turning until the circle is completed.

Look at figure 6 below to see the first step of working in a circle. From the back the needle is punched into the fabric. The beginning tag of thread remains on the back. Take the first stitch very close to the tag and up to 12 o'clock. With the bevel facing to the left, punch two or three stitches forward and very close to the tag. Turn the hoop clockwise a little so that you continue to work toward yourself. Punch in another few stitches and again turn the hoop. Continue in this manner until the required number of stitches has been worked.

Hold the thread in place, withdraw the needle and cut the thread. Turn your embroidery over and you will have formed the dearest little circle-flower. If you see that there is a hole in the middle and your flower looks like a doughnut, you can either punch some more stitches to fill in the space, or perhaps practice making some more circle-flowers, working very close to the beginning tag of the first stitch.

Effects with the basic circle

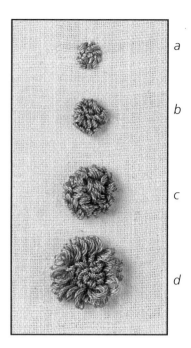

a

b

c

d

Figure 5

All samples are worked in six strands of embroidery cotton.

Sample a This is similar to figure 6 below, only the starting tag has been pulled through to the back side. It has 20 stitches in the circle. This circle can be used on the front of embroidery as an additional surface stitch.

Sample b This is the front of sample a above.

Sample c A domed circle. Ten stitches are punched in a circle with the punchneedle set at No 5 to form the centre. Mark the beginning for the next row (see figure 6, sample 1, b). Change the needle length to No 3 and work all the way around the first circle as far as the beginning mark. Change the needle to No 1. Work all the way around again.

Cut the thread. A turtle's shell, a spider's back, a teddy bear's tummy or a flower centre are examples of what can be made from a domed circle.

Sample d A small flower made with 20 stitches in a circle with the needle set at No 1. Change to No 5 to stitch all the way around. The longer loops which are formed give the appearance of petals.

Circles transformed into stunning flowers

Read Working in a Circle above.

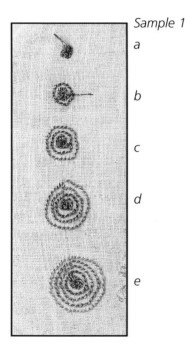

Sample 1

a

b

c

d

e

Figure 6

Sample 1a Shows the making of a circle viewed from the back. From the back the needle is punched into the fabric. The beginning tag of thread remains on the back. Take the first stitch very close to the tag and up to 12 o'clock. With the bevel facing to the left, punch 2 or 3 stitches forward and very close to the tag. Turn the hoop clockwise a little so that you continue to work toward yourself. Punch in another few stitches and again turn the hoop. Continue in this manner until 20 stitches have been worked.

Hold the thread in place, withdraw the needle, and cut the thread. Turn your embroidery over to see a small round cluster of stitches.

Sample 2a This shows the front of sample 1a.

Sample 2

a

b

c

d

e

Sample 2 Worked with 3 strands of embroidery cotton through the small needle.

Sample 1b The mark on this sample indicates where to begin and end the next round of stitches. Although it is marked in pen for clarity in this photo, I suggest that you refrain from using pen on your embroidery. It is wiser to use a water-erasable pen for simple embroidery marks.

Samples 1c, 1d, and 1e Show the remaining rows which make up the flower. There is a slight space left between each row. This space allows the loops of each row to blossom out instead of being scrunched tightly together.

Sample 2b Alter the needle to No 3. Stitch all the way around the circle

Sample 2c The needle tip is set at No 6 for this round.

Sample 2d The needle tip is set at No 9. Stitch all the way around.

Sample 2e Set the needle at No 12. Stitch all the way around.

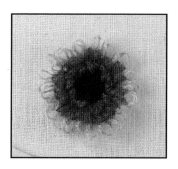

Sample 4 Worked in exactly the same way with traditional acrylic yarn.

Sample 5 The outside petals are embroidered with 4 mm silk ribbon. See Ribbon Heart project.

Special effects

There are many ways a punchneedle can be utilised to create special effects. The following samples give an insight into the diversity of the one simple stitch which makes up the beauty and variety of punchneedle embroidery.

Sample 3 Worked exactly the same as sample 2, but using six strands of embroidery cotton through the medium needle.

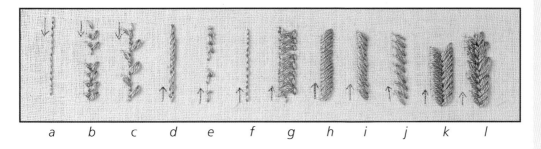

a   b   c   d   e   f   g   h   i   j   k   l

Figure 7

Sample a   Reverse punchneedle embroidery (described above).

Sample b   Closed feather stitch

Work from the front and pull the starting thread through to the back, as for reverse punchneedle embroidery. Working toward yourself, work one stitch forward. Work a stitch out and upwards to the left at approximately 45 degrees, return to the centre, and then work a stitch out and upwards to the right at approximately 45 degrees. Return to the centre and repeat the sequence.

Sample c   Open feather stitch

Work with the needle set at No 2. If the loops do not stay in place increase the length of the needle. Work from the front and pull the starting thread through to the back, as for reverse punchneedle embroidery. Work 2 straight stitches forward, then a stitch out and upwards to the left, return to the centre, then work a stitch out and upwards to the right, work 2 straight stitches forward, return to the centre and repeat the sequence.

Sample d   Overstitching reverse punchneedle embroidery

To achieve a different effect with reverse punchneedle embroidery, this stitch is very useful. Work one stitch backward and the next forward. The next stitch backwards is placed halfway along the stitch just worked. Bring another stitch forward. The next backward stitch is then placed almost into the same place as where the forward stitch left the fabric. You will have to move the forward stitch gently out of the way to make way to punch in the backward stitch. The stitches made seem to roll over where the needle penetrates the fabric so that you cannot see where the stitch went through. Working the stitches in this manner gives a thicker appearance to reverse punchneedle embroidery. The starting and ending threads are pulled through to the back of the fabric where they are trimmed.

Sample e   Snail trail

This is stitched on the front and worked backwards.

On the traced line, take a small stitch backwards. Lift the needle very slightly out of the fabric, skim the needle tip over the stitch just worked and take a small horizontal stitch immediately to the right. Punch the needle into the fabric. Lift the needle tip over the stitch just made and re-insert it just above the first stitch onto the traced line.

Sample f Backwards reverse punchneedle embroidery

On the front of the design, work reverse punchneedle embroidery backwards, away from yourself. Doing reverse punchneedle embroidery this way gives a higher, denser appearance to the stitch. The difference in appearance is very subtle but with certain threads it becomes noticeable and interesting.

Sample g Herringbone punch

Depending on the width of the area to be embroidered, set the needle length at No 2 or 3 so that the loops hold in place.

Work backwards. Begin with a small running stitch backward. Then take the needle to the left at a slight upward angle. Bring a small running stitch directly forward. Take the needle to the right at a slight upward angle. Lift the needle over the stitch just made and bring a small running stitch directly forward. Then take the needle to the left at a slight upward angle.

Repeat until the required area is completed.

Samples h and i Satin stitch

This is worked from the front with long straight stitches which can be angled either to the left or the right to give effect. With this stitch it is important that the needle tip is long enough so that the punched loops stay in place on the back. Start with the needle set at No 2; if the stitches do not hold, alter the length and keep a check on the back to see if the loops are long enough to hold in place. Work the stitches close together so that the threads rest on each other to give a beautiful raised satin stitch effect known widely in traditional hand embroidery.

Sample j Textured satin stitch

This is worked in the same way as satin stitch except that the stitches are not punched so close together. It is possible to see where the stitches cross each other. It is used with great effect for leaves.

Sample k Open leaf satin stitch

(This is also shown in figure 18.)

This is a great alternative for embroidering a leaf and gives quite a different look when compared to a leaf worked in satin stitch (see figure 8).

This stitch is worked backwards. Take a stitch to the left and return to the centre. Take a stitch to the right and return to the centre. Continue in this manner until the required area is filled in. If forming a leaf, the stitches are made shorter as the tip is approached. Depending on the look desired, take each stitch up at an angle and work the stitches close together or alternatively further apart to give the appearance of a fern leaf.

Sample l Open leaf satin stitch with reverse punchneedle embroidery.

Worked as above, but making the stitches to the left and the right erratic in length for a different finish. When the top or tip of the area is reached, stitch forward through the centre with small stitches in reverse punchneedle embroidery.

To embroider a leaf

Figure 8

Start with the needle set at No 2. If however, the loops do not stay in place, increase the needle length.

When working a leaf in satin stitch, always work from the base of the leaf to the tip. The first part of this stitching is worked backwards, away from you. Turn the bevel of the needle tip slightly in your finger tips, away from the left to about 10 o'clock. Glide the back of the needle just along the former stitch. This helps to lay the stitch down smoothly. Take a stitch from the centre to the right and back to the centre. The stitching may begin to look too horizontal, in which case to get an upward angle punch a few stitches into the centre, in exactly the same hole, taking each outside stitch a little further up. Make the stitches shorter toward the tip of the leaf. At the very tip, take 2 or 3 small backward reverse punchneedle embroidery stitches to form a nice point.

The angle of the bevel when punching forward is not directly to the left, but turned in the fingers to about 8 o'clock. Moving forward, punch 2 or 3 small stitches directly over the stitches just worked. Commence stitching forward, working out to the left and then into the centre until the leaf is completed. The stitches on the left side of the leaf sit differently to those on the right.

Towards each leaf tip, change to a shorter needle length to prevent a lot of bulk from long loops forming at the back. Alter the length of the needle on its return. Pull the starting and finishing threads to the back of the work and trim.

Meandering stitch

Figure 9

The meandering stitch is exactly that! It is simply reverse punchneedle embroidery meandering backwards, forwards, in and out and round about, leaving a delicate outline over the surface of the fabric. It is a useful fill-in surface stitch which can add great interest to a design.

Where a large area is to be filled in with loops which are not close together, such as in the background of The Flower Garden, punch from the back in the manner of the meandering stitch and the loops on the front will be erratic and not as uniform as when rows are worked.

Forming the perfect point

a   b   c

Figure 10

Forming the perfect point can be of great consternation to the punchneedle embroiderer, but there are a couple of ways to achieve perfection! Common areas of concern are the tip of a petal, pointy animal ears and the corners of a square.

If you merrily punch away, get to a corner, stitch around it and continue along the other side, you will end up with an overhanging stitch looking quite out of place, as in sample c.

Work along the outline tracing on the back. Stitch to the tip of a point. For the very last punched stitch at the tip, deliberately angle the needle tip inwards and actually change the slant of the needle from about the usual 60 degrees to nearer 30 degrees.

Punch the last stitch made at the very tip. The next stitch along the second side is made longer and is punched at least one or two stitch lengths from the tip— see sample a. This means that on the front there is not a bunch of loops forming at the tip, all vying for a place to sit. Check on the front. It may be that a few stitches need to be undone and re-worked to achieve the perfect point, as in sample b.

Another trick of mine is to 'use the finger'. Let me explain. The finger becomes a valuable tool in punchneedle embroidery. Where there is an unruly loop, such as on a point or elsewhere on the embroidery, with your index finger on the back of the piece under the embroidery, scratch the stitch producing the unruly loop, which will nearly always get the loop to settle into place.

Another way to a perfect point

The Handstand Clown (page 105) has white daisies on his trousers. To look good the tips of the daisy petals need to be sharp. As shown in figure 11, there is a simple method to accomplish this. (There is a diagram in the Handstand Clown project which explains this in a slightly different manner. Both methods have the same outcome.)

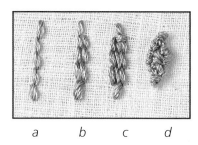

a   b   c   d

Figure 11

The stitches in samples a, b, and c have been exaggerated for clarity.

Sample a Work from the back. Stitch as many stitches forward as required for the size of the daisy. There are 5 stitches in the first row of the petal in this sample. Leave the needle in the fabric. Turn the hoop.

Sample b The first stitch forward and on the left of the initial row is worked down at an angle and placed near where the last stitch of the previous row emerged. Work 4 stitches forwards. This means that there is only one loop at the tip on the other side of the embroidery. Leave the needle in the fabric.

Sample c Turn the hoop. Take a horizontal stitch across the first row of stitching. Work 3 forward stitches.

Sample d This shows the front of the completed petal and the effectiveness of producing an almost perfect point.

And yet another way to a perfect point

There is a little bit of cheating with this! Often when a punch-embroidered appliqué has been cut out, points such as a duck's beak, a fish's fin or tail are not as crisp as they might be. This is probably because the outside row of stitching has not been worked closely enough together. An easy remedy is to put a small quantity of glue between the thumb and index finger, take the point and gently squeeze it, leaving a fine residue of glue which sharpens the point.

Star flowers

These are perfect little fill-in flowers. You can see them in The Flower Garden (page 129).

Figure 12

For surface embellishment the star is worked on the front of the fabric. Set the needle tip just sufficiently long enough to enable the loops to stay in place. Commence in the centre. Punch a stitch into the centre. Make a stitch outwards to the required length and then make another stitch back into the centre. Work 5 petals for the daisy, taking each stitch in and out. Pull the beginning and ending threads to the back.

Sample a Worked with three strands of embroidery cotton.

Sample b Worked with six strands of embroidery cotton.

Stripes

How do you get the perfect stripe?

sample 1

sample 2

a   b

Figure 13

In punchneedle embroidery, stripes can end up either embroidered with perfect delineation between the colours, or with the colours all jumbled together. There is one simple way to achieve the perfect stripe. Simply leave a space between each row.

Samples 1a & 1b Show stripes where the rows have been stitched very close together. The loops on the front become intermingled with each so that it really seems that there are no stripes.

Samples 2a & 2b Show how stripes take on a definite line when a space has been left between the rows.

Outlines

sample 1

sample 2

a   b

Figure 14

This technique involves working reverse punchneedle embroidery around areas in your embroidery to emphasise their outline. This technique can be seen with great effect in the project Nasturtiums, where the flowers and leaves are completed with a row of reverse punchneedle embroidery around them. The samples here are not quite as effective as the project, but demonstrate the effectiveness of the technique quite adequately. Knowing this technique and using it in certain areas of your floral embroidery will be valuable when you want to add more definition to an area of your work.

Sample 1a Shows a small circle worked with three strands of thread with the needle set at No 1 and 20 stitches worked in a circle. Where you are embroidering a fine piece it can look so much better if you are able to tighten the circle.

Sample 1b Shows how tightening a circle is easily done by adding a row of reverse punchneedle embroidery at the very base of the loops on the front of the embroidery.

Sample 2a Worked with the punchneedle set at No 6, showing a circle where the loops are spread out.

Sample 2b A second row of loops has been worked around the first row with the needle set at No 1. This second row holds the first row up and prevents the loops from spreading too wide.

Sculpting

This technique is absolutely wonderful for getting deep, rich and luxurious textures into punchneedle embroidery. Although ideal for bears and other animals, there are many other areas where it can be incorporated, such as the centres of flowers, brooches (see Scarf Toggles, page 124)—and it makes fabulous looking moss (see Bush Floor, page 182.

Figure 15

These samples have been embroidered with acrylic yarn through the medium needle.

Sample 1 Shows the grid marked ready for embroidering.

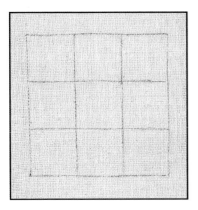

Sample 2 Shows the embroidery from the back. Note the space left between each punched area. The space is very important for sculpting.

Sample 4 Worked with the needle set at No 10. You can see in this sample that the right-hand square at the bottom has the loops embroidered but not cut. The other two areas have had the loops cut open. It is absolutely necessary that as each row of loops is worked they are cut open. Working more than 2 rows without cutting the loops will make it almost impossible to cut at all, as the loops tend to get tangled and caught up with each other.

Sample 3 Shows the finished embroidery from the front. The needle was set at No 1. Leaving the space between each area prevents the loops from the neighbouring areas becoming intermingled. The squares are almost perfectly delineated.

Sample 5 To shape a sculpted area after the loops have been cut is very exciting.
Cut the *outside edges* of the loops ruthlessly back to the tracing lines on the fabric to give shape to the design. These

edges are either cut straight to form a square (as in this sample) or the edges are gently shaped into a curve to become rounded like the Handstand Clown's balancing ball (see page 105).

You can, however, initially embroider the outside row with a much shorter loop length which assists in giving form to the shape you are creating. These shorter loops may not even need to be cut, depending on the effect that you wish to achieve.

The lines delineating areas inside a design do not need to be cut so radically and only very gentle sculpting and shaping is required.

In places where too much has been cut or the finish looks patchy, punch in extra loops and then trim them.

Where some loops escape the cutting process this can actually add character to a finished embroidery. The cut loops change colour and depending on the thread used they can become richer and more vibrant. The uncut loops remain a softer colour and add a fleck of more subtle colour into the plushness of the design.

Very fine punchneedle embroidery

Figure 16

An example of this technique can be seen with the Magical Miniature Carpet (page 143).

This sample has been embroidered with a very fine punchneedle through which only one strand of thread can be passed. The 1 cm (⅜ in) square outline was made following the technique described for straightening the grain of the fabric (page 56). The pile depth on the very fine needle was set at 6 mm (¼ in). The sample shown used 1.85 metres (approximately 73 inches) of thread. There are around 435 stitches embroidered into this small square.

Blending threads

Figure 17

Using different tones of the one colour through the punchneedle is just another exciting addition to punchneedle embroidery.

In Butterflies (page 76), the pretty colours on the larger butterfly have been blended using a mixture of six strands of thread in three tones of pink; the smaller is worked with blends of three strands in the same pinks.

Blending six strands of thread

A = darkest tone, B = medium tone and C =lightest tone
The first (outer) row is worked with 6 strands of the darkest colour.
The next row, 4 strands of the dark with 2 strands of the medium.

The next row, 4 strands of medium with 2 strands of dark
Follow this with 6 strands of medium.
Take 4 strands of medium and 2 strands of light.
The next row, 4 strands of light with 2 strands of medium.
Finally, use 6 strands of light.
To avoid distinct lines between colour changes, overlap the rows by punching a few stitches of the adjacent shade into the next shade.

Blending three strands of thread

Blending 6 strands of thread

6A	4A 2B	4B 2A	6B	4B 2C	4C 2B	6C

A = 604 dark pink
B = 605 medium pink
C = 606 light pink

Blending 3 strands of thread

3A	2A 1B	2B 1A	3B	2B 1C	2C 1B	3C

A = 604 dark pink
B = 605 medium pink
C = 606 light pink

Other stitches
Open textured satin stitch

Figure 18

This is explained in sample 7, k. It is a very effective manner in which to embroider a leaf. A number of leaves have been worked like this in Circle Upon a Circle (page 166).

Going dotty!

Figure 19

This sample demonstrates how to put different coloured dots over an embroidered area. The heart has been worked with the punchneedle set at No 1. To add the dots the needle length was altered to No 2. With the needle at No 1 there is insufficient length of loop to show through the thickly textured background embroidery, as can be seen on the left side of the heart. The right side has been embroidered with the needle set at No 2 thereby making the dots more obvious. It is important to hold on to the thread where it exits the fabric before punching in the next stitch. If the thread is not held in place the loop is sometimes pulled out as the needle is slid along the thread to punch in the next dot. (Specific instructions are given with a number of designs; for example, Giraffes)

Cutting loops— changing colours

a   b   c

Figure 20

When loops are cut a change of colour often occurs. This may be a slight or a dramatic change depending on the type and colour of the thread being used.

Sample a Traditional punchneedle embroidery acrylic yarn has been cut here. A lovely velvety appearance has been achieved with not a great deal of colour change.

Sample b Satin acrylic yarn. Where the loops have been cut there is a dramatic change to the colour with a rich intensity giving a luxurious finish.

Sample c Madeira 6-stranded embroidery thread is shown in this sample. There is a marked colour change affording lushness to the cut loops.

The knot-like stitch

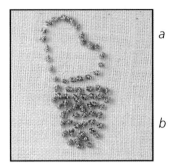

a

b

Figure 21

The tiny knot-like stitch only looks like a little knot if it is worked with a short needle tip. This is something that you will need to experiment with—the shorter the loop the more knot-like the stitch will appear. However, if the loops are too short they will not stay in place. When using the small Ultra-Punch needle with the needle tip set at No 1, slip a small length of plastic about 2–3 mm (approximately ⅛ in) long over the needle tip, pushing it up the needle past the eye until it is against the plastic casing. This shortens the needle tip which in turn will shorten the loop made on the front and it will look just like a tiny knot. Practise a little to get a suitable length for the knot-like loop. Work from the back of the work, punching in loops approximately 2 mm apart.

Sample a If you are doing an outline, follow the tracing of the outline with the loops spaced at 2 mm.

Sample b If an area is to be filled in with knot-like loops, to get a good overall coverage work the same way as the Meandering stitch (from the back, figure 9, Stitch Glossary) and punch the loops far enough apart so they also resemble individual knots.

Zigzag stitch

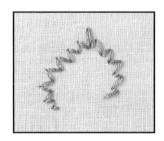

Figure 22

The zigzag effect is used in one small area of Circle Upon a Circle (page 166). Set the needle at No 2 or 3. Embroider from the front of the piece and work in a zigzag motion. This decorative stitch adds another effect which gives further interest to your embroidery.

Silk ribbon work Flower

Figure 23

This flower has been embroidered with 13 mm (½ in) silk ribbon using the

Dancing Ribbon needle, which uses widths of ribbon from 7 mm (just over ¼ in) to 13 mm (½ in). The flowers are made in the same manner as those in Figure 6 above. The lengths of the loops are of course much longer. The finished width of the flower in this sample is approximately 70 mm (2 ¾ in). It is interesting to note that although there is very little stitching on the back it gives rise to a full, sumptuous bloom on the front. There is a diagram for this technique in the project A Promise of Summer.

Tapering spike

a   b

Figure 24

The tapering spike can emulate many flowers, such as lavender, wisteria, delphinium, depending on the colour chosen. It is a great way to fill in around a bunch of flowers, as seen in A Promise of Summer.

Sample a Shows how few stitches are embroidered on the back. The embroidery for the first section is worked in small zigzags across the traced line and the end stitches are worked in a straight line.

Sample b Shows how full blown the loops become.

There is a diagram for this technique in A Promise of Summer.

Braid making

Braids are used as a delightful finishing touch in a number of projects. They can be made in two different ways, by the finger method or with a braid-making tool.

The advantages of the finger method, whereby threads are twisted together with the fingers, are one, it is a relaxing activity and two, the twisted threads do not readily unravel. Braids made by the finger method stay twisted when let go and are finer in appearance.

A braid maker, known as a 'Spinster', quickens the process a great deal. This tool looks something like a small hand-held drill used for woodwork, but where the drill piece fits there is a small hook. Braids made with the Spinster may unravel when let go, so tie a knot at the end of the braid as soon as the Spinster has finished its twisting act.

Finger method

To make a braid of a given length by this method you need to start with threads that are about 3 times longer. To make a braid 18 cm (7 in) long, as required for the Christmas Decorations on page 99, for example, you need to start with threads 54 cm (21 in) long.

Cut four or six lengths of the chosen thread/yarn. Knot them together at one end. Divide the threads into two equal amounts.

Hold the knotted end in the left hand or secure it to a firm surface with a pin.

Take the threads on the right side between the right-hand index finger and the thumb and twist them tightly to the right.

Pass the right-hand threads over the left ones; now take the second group of threads between the index finger and thumb of the right hand and twist these to the right.

Reverse the way of holding the thread if left handed.

Repeat this process until you have a length of braid sufficient for your purpose. Tie a knot at the end of the braid.

Spinster method

This is a little tricky at first, but worth persevering with as you can make beautiful braids quite easily after a little practice. The threads required for a given length of braid by this method need to 2.5–3 times as long. Again using the 18 cm (20 in) length required for the Christmas decorations as an example, cut four or six pieces of yarn each 45–54 cm (50–60 in) long. Tie them together with a knot *at each end*.

Divide the threads into two equal amounts, and place one end over a cup hook or something similar.

Place the hook of the braid maker into the other end and pull the threads out to their full length.

Wind the handle of the braid maker until the thread is twisted very tightly. Relax the thread a little (just a little) to check if it is twisting upon itself. Wind a little further if it is not.

Hold the end where the braid maker is attached in the left hand and remove the braid maker from the braid with the right hand, taking extreme care not to relax the twisted thread. This can become quite a challenge. Either keep your arms fully outstretched so that the braid cannot begin to untwist before it is intended, or engage someone to help!

With the right hand place the hook of the braid maker halfway along the length of the twisted thread, at the same time keeping the twisted cord straight. Take the free end up to meet the knotted end on the cup hook. The braid maker will hang on the twisted thread.

Remove the braid from the cup hook and place the two knotted ends together. Let the threads twist upon themselves, with the braid maker forming a weight and spinning as the threads are twisting.

When the twisting motion has finished, hold the braid and tie another knot at the end with the knots, then remove braid maker. There will be a small loop where the hook was.

And you have your braid!

Stitch key

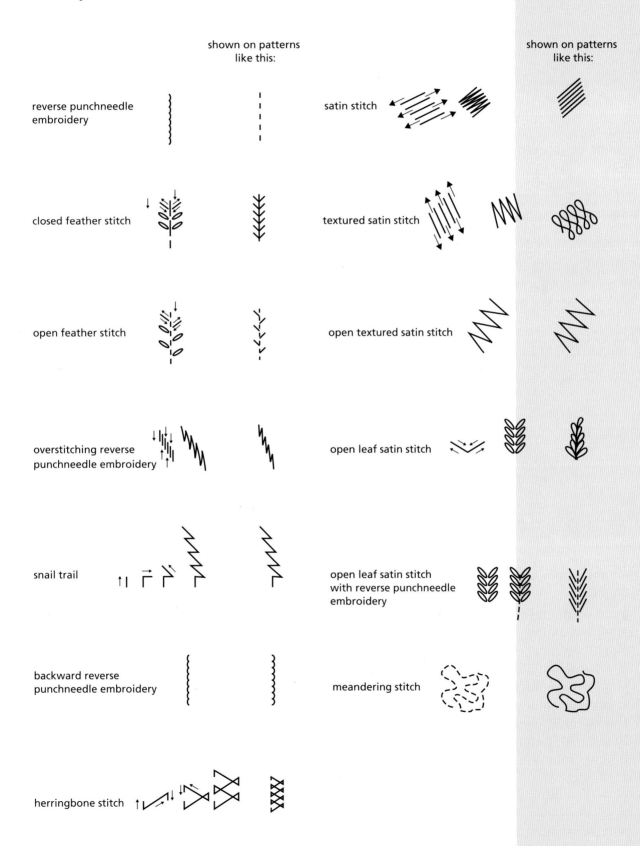

shown on patterns like this:

shown on patterns like this:

reverse punchneedle embroidery

satin stitch

closed feather stitch

textured satin stitch

open feather stitch

open textured satin stitch

overstitching reverse punchneedle embroidery

open leaf satin stitch

snail trail

open leaf satin stitch with reverse punchneedle embroidery

backward reverse punchneedle embroidery

meandering stitch

herringbone stitch

4 Materials, equipment and basic techniques

Fabrics

A tightly woven fabric is required for punchneedle embroidery. It is important to know and understand that it is primarily the weave of the fabric that holds the embroidered loops in place. Punchneedles may damage some fabrics and care needs to be taken when choosing a fabric to work on.

I use many types of fabric, although experience has shown me that fabrics which contain a proportion of polyester give the best results. Other fabrics can be used, but be aware that there are many qualities and types. Some experimentation is needed and it is great fun to find fabrics that work beautifully with punchneedle embroidery.

A perfect fabric for punchneedle embroidery is American weaver's cloth (also known as Candlelite), which is composed of polyester and cotton. In Australia I have tried a range of lovely polyester viscose fabrics and I am currently using a fabric which is a poly/viscose/flax blend made in Australia. I have successfully used doctor's flannel, some blanketing wools, dressmaker's satin, various polycottons, a delightful silk noil and other fabrics. It is a thrill to find a fabric which works beautifully and which allows my needles to dance.

Many tightly woven fabrics have a certain amount of stretch to them. Check this characteristic before proceeding with a particular fabric because, depending on the direction of the stretch, whether it is along the warp or weft, it can distort the shape of a design. The warp is the lengthwise fibres following the selvedge, whereas the weft is made up of threads crossing from side to side. (Remember: weft goes 'weft to wite'.) If a design of a bear, for instance, is traced onto fabric with a lot of stretch, the finished animal might be long and skinny, or short and fat, depending on which way of the stretch the design was traced and embroidered onto the fabric.

It is only necessary to pre-wash fabric which may have a tendency to shrink if the finished item is likely to be washed, such as a piece of clothing. The sizing present in unwashed fabrics appears not to damage the punchneedles.

Testing a sample of fabric before starting on a project can reduce the risk of failure and frustration. Place a sample of the chosen fabric in a hoop and work some stitches with the punchneedle and thread that you intend using. Undo the trial stitching and have a good look at the fabric to see if it is damaged. If you can coax the warp and weft back into place with a fingernail where the punchneedle has made an opening, and the surrounding fibres have not been damaged, then the fabric is generally suitable to use. If the fabric is visibly damaged, an iron-on woven interfacing applied to the back of it will strengthen it, and usually the embroidery can proceed without further concern.

The stretchy fabrics used for sweatshirts need to have an iron-on woven interfacing bonded onto the back before commencing the embroidery. An alternative to working directly onto this type of fabric is to use the appliqué method, which eliminates the need to work on the actual stretch fabric. (See Appliqué, page 59.)

The appliqué method is also an ideal alternative to working directly onto wool blanketing or terry towelling. The bulk of thick woollen blanketing makes it difficult to get this fabric sufficiently taut in the hoop to work satisfactorily. However, there are so many types of blanketing that you need to have a practice with any blanketing you have chosen. If your blanket fabric holds the loops, there is no reason not to work directly onto it. If it is too open in weave, the loops cannot stay in place.

I do not advocate applying iron-on interfacing to the back of woollen blanketing, as the heat required for bonding may damage the wool fibres. You can, however, stitch a woven fabric onto the back. Use short running stitches (with a sewing needle and thread) and stitch in a grid with the rows about 6 mm (¼ in) apart. When you have finished the embroidery the stitches are removed and the backing fabric is cut carefully away to the punched outline.

Always be aware of the thickness of the fabric and the need to have it taut in the hoop. Wool flannel, also known as doctor's flannel, is not as thick as wool blanketing. It is expensive, but it is a joy to work on. I have successfully used this with both tapestry and crewel wool through the appropriate punchneedle.

There are so many beautiful fabrics to choose from and often it is only through experimenting that you will find which fabrics work more successfully than others.

Iron-on interfacing

There are many types of iron-on woven interfacing. Some types are very fine and filmy while others are more like muslin. They have a special coating on the back which melts when heat is applied and bonds onto the main fabric.

If you have chosen a fabric which is too fine and fragile in nature for the size of punchneedle you intend to use, you will have to consider using interfacing. Not all fabric will require it. Test your chosen fabric—if the punchneedle damages the fibres, then interfacing needs to be used.

It is best to use a woven interfacing as opposed to the knitted varieties available for dressmaking. Before ironing the interfacing into place, check that there are no bits of fluff or hair caught between the two layers, as these can show up noticeably through some fabrics and spoil the look of a finished piece of work. It is necessary to bond the interfacing very well to the fabric. When the backed fabric is pulled very tightly in a hoop the

Equipment used in punchneedle embroidery

interfacing, if not adhered strongly, can come apart from the fabric. When this happens any loops worked can be lost between the two layers.

Equipment

Scissors

Small, sharp, pointed embroidery scissors are essential. With sharp, pointy scissors, threads on the back can be cut close to the fabric. Blunt, rough scissors can very easily pull out worked areas. It is ideal to have two pairs of scissors, one for cutting glued ends and a good sharp pair for trimming and sculpting.

Tweezers

Tweezers are invaluable and most useful when working reverse punchneedle embroidery, where the beginning and ending threads must be pulled to the back of the fabric.

Craft glue

There are many types of fabric glue available. Choose acid-free glue and look for qualities such as it being clear, soft and pliable when it dries. You Can Wash It craft glue from Craftsmart is excellent. It is used to seal the cut edges of appliqué work and can be lightly smeared onto the back of a completed piece of embroidery to give added security to the formed loops to prevent them being accidentally pulled out. It can also be used on the beginning and end of threads to prevent them slipping through to the front.

Pressure-sensitive craft glue

This glue is applied to the back of an appliqué design and left to dry until it is tacky. The appliqué can then be pressed onto a garment where it remains secure until removed. The tackiness lasts for many applications before the glue needs to be replenished. Using this type of Off'N'On glue from Craftsmart gives great versatility to an appliqué design when it is not necessary to have it adhered permanently.

Ruler

A small ruler is often required for measuring needle lengths and the small pieces of plastic tubing used for altering the length of the needle tip on punchneedles that do not have a gauge or settings for this purpose. Most rulers have the measured markings beginning a few millimetres in from the end. If a small plastic ruler is available, cut this end off with an old pair of scissors (not good sewing scissors) so that the first measurements are at the very end of the ruler. This makes measuring needle length so much easier.

Crochet hook

A very fine steel 0.75 (No. 6) crochet hook is useful to pull any long loops or ends that show up on the front of the embroidery through to the back. Refrain from cutting any threads on the front of

the work as threads change colour when cut and leave dark marks which show up dramatically on the finished work. See figure 20 in the Stitch Glossary. Be extremely careful using the hook, as it is easy to get it caught in the thread and to pull out too many stitches. When retracting the crochet hook do so with a gentle, twisting action.

Light-box

A light-box is really handy. This is a box with a glass top under which is a light. When a design and fabric are placed over the lit box, the outline of the design readily shows through the fabric for ease of tracing. However, if you do not have access to a light-box then a well-lit window works equally well. Hold or tape the traced pattern with the fabric over it, onto a window. With the light shining through it is easy to see the outline which needs to be traced. Use a sharp lead pencil, water-erasable pen or a heat-transfer pen.

Heat-transfer pen

An easy way to get a design onto fabric is with a heat-transfer pen. The design is traced onto tracing or computer paper. The traced image is turned over and placed into position onto the back of the fabric. It is then heated with an iron set at the appropriate heat for the fabric being used. The hotter the iron, the darker the imprint. If a light imprint is required, apply less heat. Refrain from sliding the iron over the back of the paper as the tracing may smudge if the paper moves at all. When ironed onto the fabric the tracing will show in the reverse. When the traced design is worked from the back in punchneedle embroidery the completed piece, which is viewed from the front, will be facing the same way as the original drawing. Store the tracing when finished as it can be used quite a number of times before the transferred design becomes too light. Make sure the pen cap is placed on the pen when not in use. Like all felt-tipped pens it will dry out if left uncovered.

Iron-on transfer pencils

Iron-on transfer pencils are an easy way of transferring a design onto fabric but not quite as clean and crisp as a heat-transfer pen. The design is traced onto tracing paper with the pencil, positioned tracing side down onto the back of the fabric, and ironed over with the iron set at an appropriate heat for the fabric. The drawn design becomes imprinted onto the fabric. The image traced onto the tracing paper is ironed onto the back of the fabric in reverse. However, the embroidery on the front of the fabric will be facing the same way as the initial tracing. A minor problem with the iron-on transfer pencil is the difficulty of achieving a truly fine line. Sharpen the pencil frequently and wipe the tip before using, as granules of colour can fall on to your work.

Water-erasable pen

Water-erasable pen lines are ideal for marking an image onto fabric where a permanent image is not desired. A design traced onto the front of the fabric with this pen in preparation for reverse punchneedle embroidery can easily be

removed with a damp cloth. Some types of pens are available with a fine tip at one end and a thick tip at the other. There is speculation in some quarters as to how the ink residue may affect fabric years from now.

Dressmaker's carbon

White or coloured dressmaker's carbon is useful where there is a need to transfer a design onto black or a dark fabric as the design outlines can readily be seen. The marks can be removed with a damp cloth.

Pellon

Pellon is a soft, thin wadding used in quilting. It is ideal to use with a completed piece of punchneedle embroidery, particularly where reverse punchneedle embroidery has been incorporated. With reverse punchneedle embroidery the punched loops are formed on the back of the embroidery. During framing when the fabric is stretched by the framer, the loops bulge out through the fabric and look unsightly in the finished and framed piece. Place pellon under the fabric before stretching it and the loops nestle into the softness and 'disappear'.

Transferring the design

There are many methods to transfer a design onto fabric such as the use of a light-box, heat-transfer pens, water-erasable pens or dressmaker's carbon. There will be instances where one method prevails over another. For example, a light-box will be of no use when transferring a design onto black fabric. The preferred method here is to use a coloured dressmaker's carbon.

An extremely important consideration when transferring a design onto fabric is that it is placed on the straight of the fabric.

Marking the straight grain of the fabric

Marking the straight grain allow you to position a design accurately.

This technique is particularly useful when a precise square design is being worked, the Magical Miniature Carpet being an excellent example. Marking is done with a crochet hook, with the fabric stretched very tightly in the hoop. Place the back (the ball) of the hook onto the fabric between two rows of weave. Press down and drag the ball firmly between the two rows. This separates the fibres slightly and leaves a mark which is easy to see and to work along. This line may look slightly crooked when stretched in the hoop but it straightens when the fabric is removed from the hoop.

Hoop techniques

With punchneedle embroidery it is very important to have the fabric stretched as tightly as possible in a hoop. When the fabric is drum-tight, the weave of the fabric is opened up and this allows the punchneedle to find its way easily between the fibres.

The punchneedle technique of embroidery is also more enjoyable when the fabric is tight in the hoop. The needle can find its way easily between the fibres, the loops stay in place, progress is made and everything works beautifully. Working with fabric which is not pulled taut means that it is more difficult to punch the needle through the fabric. As well, a great deal of stress is placed on your wrist, which can prove painful over time—but most importantly, the loops do not readily stay in place, causing one to wonder if there is something wrong with the punchneedle.

There are many types of embroidery hoops available but few will hold the fabric tight enough. The smaller the hoop size the tighter the fabric can be pulled,

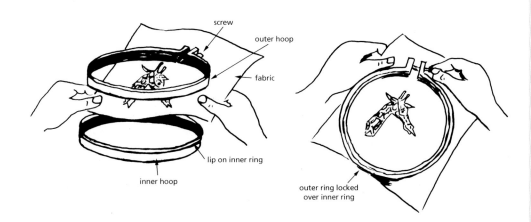

Placing fabric into the hoop

The fabric must be stretched taut in the hoop

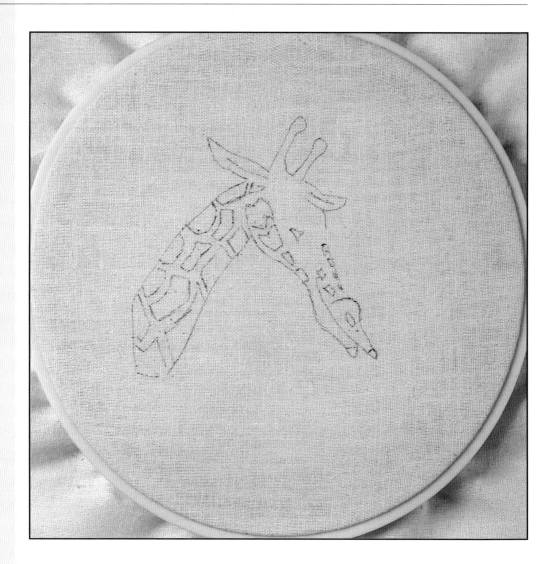

without much effort. When a larger hoop is used it will require more effort to get the fabric tight enough.

The ideal hoop is a plastic lip-lock hoop. This hoop has an inner ring with a lip, and an outer ring with a nut for tightening. When the lip on the inner hoop is positioned up and over the outer ring and the nut is done up tightly, the fabric is held secure and very taut (drum tight) which is the optimum for punchneedle embroidery.

Be aware that it is possible to have the nut done up very tightly and the fabric still not tight in the hoop. It is a step-by-step process to tighten the fabric. Turn the assembled hoop and fabric so that the fabric is resting on the table top. Put your fingers inside the hoop and your thumbs over the fabric on the outside. Work around the hoop, pulling the fabric tight at every quarter turn. Tighten the nut after each turn. Repeat the whole process three or four times until the fabric is drum tight and the nut cannot be tightened further. And for one final measure, pick the hoop up, turn it over and give a jolly good tug to the fabric all the way around.

The lip-lock hoop which is nearly always sold with a punchneedle set generally has a small nut for tightening.

This is quite hard to get hold of and for people with sore, weak or arthritic fingers is often difficult to tighten. A brass nut called the Perfect nut is available to replace the existing nut. The Perfect nut can be tightened with fingers, a coin or a small screwdriver.

The screw on some lip-lock hoops occasionally has insufficient thread to allow the hoop to be adequately opened. This problem can be overcome by removing the nut and placing a 'pony' bead on the screw. Replace the nut and tighten it as much as possible against the pony bead.

If great difficulty is being experienced in getting the fabric tight enough, tighten it as much as possible and then place the assembled hoop over a pudding basin, dessert bowl or wooden bowl which fits inside the hoop to work the embroidery. As the work is being pushed down over the bowl and the pressure from the bowl pushes up, added tension is given to the fabric. Be careful though not to punch the needle into the sides of the bowl, which may damage the tip.

At times the outline of a design can become distorted when the fabric is stretched in the hoop. Pull the fabric in the hoop to make the design as near to the original tracing as is possible.

Size of fabric

The fabric needs to be large enough to fit into the hoop and leave sufficient allowance to be pulled on when tightening the fabric.

As it is necessary to frequently turn the work over to check (and, of course, to admire what you have achieved),

working with a large piece of fabric can be a nuisance—it often gets you into all sorts of trouble, catching on things, knocking things onto the floor and just simply getting in the way. If it is necessary to work with a large piece of fabric, roll the edges and secure with safety pins to make working easier and safer.

If you have a special piece of fabric which is too small to fit into the hoop, stitch calico borders onto it to make it large enough.

Doughnuts and dirty marks

There is one small drawback to using the special lip-lock hoop with the fabric pulled drum tight. The hoop sometimes leaves the imprint of a circular mark on the fabric that is particularly difficult to remove. To prevent such marks developing consider the use of a 'doughnut' or, possibly, a larger hoop so that any marks will be outside the area of fabric to be seen when finished. It is possible to remove such marks by steaming with an iron or pressing with a Rajah cloth (a chemically treated ironing cloth). A pressing cloth moistened with white vinegar and water can also be useful. Always remove any dirty marks before pressing, as the heat from an iron can set them permanently. Occasionally, however, it is impossible to remove the impressed mark, which is especially disappointing when a great deal of work has gone into a project.

If the design you are working on is larger than the hoop size, and you have to

A doughnut protects the fabric from dirty marks and hoop impressions

work in sections, when you move the hoop you will have to place it over some of the embroidery, such as in the Nasturtiums project. It is normally quite safe to do so as long as you have used good quality threads. When the hoop is removed the stitching will be flattened under it. These flat areas can be fluffed up by scratching on the loops with your fingernail or by holding a steam iron over the affected area in the same way that one raises the plush of velvet.

A doughnut is a square of calico or similar fabric the same size as the fabric being embroidered with the centre cut

out to reveal the design, placed over the front of it before the two pieces of fabric are assembled together in the hoop. You work on the embroidery through the hole in the doughnut. A second doughnut can be placed at the back of the fabric to further assist in softening the impression of the hoop.

The doughnut protects the fabric from impressions in the fabric caused by a tight hoop, and from the dirty marks resulting from the natural oils in your skin, especially when the hoop nut is being constantly tightened and the thumb rubs upon the fabric. One needs to be aware that these dirty marks occur far too easily, are cumulative and are often not noticed until the piece is nearly completed or being prepared for framing. This is particularly the case with a piece such as Cream on Cream, which is mostly worked from the front of the fabric.

Where the hoop is not big enough and needs to be moved during embroidery, a doughnut will protect already embroidered areas. It will need to be repositioned whenever the work is moved.

Dirty marks can usually be removed by gently rubbing the area with a clean cloth moistened with water with the addition of a little white vinegar or a very small amount of soap. Gently rub the offending mark. Move the cloth around to a clean spot, moisten it with clean water and gently rub the area to dry it.

Appliqué

There are many places where appliquéing a design to a background is beneficial. I often work designs onto a piece of fabric, cut them out and attach them elsewhere. The butterflies in the Butterflies project have been made like this. The appliqué method is ideal if you want to embellish a stretch-knit sweat shirt instead of embroidering directly onto it. Appliqués can give extra dimension to the look of a finished piece of work.

Embroider the design. Remove the fabric from the hoop and stretch it in all directions to straighten the embroidery. Glue over the back of the completed design and about 6 mm (¼ in) onto the fabric all around it. Be sure to impregnate the fabric with glue as some fabrics can fray when cut if there is not sufficient glue to prevent this. Allow to dry. Cut the embroidered design away from the fabric with a small, sharp pair of scissors. Take care not to cut any loops; however, if you do, simply put a little bit of glue on a pin tip and press this onto the cut loop, pushing the loop back into place.

To make it less obvious that the design has been appliquéd, wherever possible work the design on a background fabric similar in colour to the outside row of stitching. For example, work on black fabric if the outside edge of the embroidery is worked in black, as in the Giraffe project. If a pale fabric has been used, the pale cut edge will be more obvious and may detract from the finished item.

You can also paint the outside edge to match before cutting and then touch up the areas which haven't taken the paint when it was cut, but note that sometimes the glue used on the back will prevent the fabric taking on the paint. I use various colouring methods: try watercolour pencils, a matching felt-tip pen or fabric paints.

In some situations, to counteract the problem of the colour of the base fabric showing, it may be simpler to work the outside edge at a longer loop length.

The embroidered cut-out can be permanently attached with You Can Wash It craft glue. Alternatively, pressure-sensitive Off'N'On glue can be used if the cut-out is not required to be attached permanently. With this glue you can wear your beautiful creations on a range of different clothing or accessories. They make lovely gifts for friends. For more detail see Craft Glue and Pressure-sensitive Glue (page 52-53), and The Use of Glue (page 26).

Creating backgrounds

Paints and pencils

A painted wash background can enhance a design. There are many excellent books available on fabric painting which have some stunning ideas. Just to help you along a little here are a few hints:

- There are many ways to create a background colour with paint such as Jo Sonja paints. The addition of textile medium, a fixative to make the paint permanent, is required where the embroidery will be laundered.
- Rexel Derwent Watercolour pencils are an easy way to lay some colour onto fabric, but may fade in time as there is no fixative.
- When using paints or pencils err on the side of a pale wash first. Add further colour to darken the area to achieve your desired effect.
- Slightly moistening the area before applying any paint gives a softer look.
- It is preferable to apply the paint before commencing the embroidery.

Iron-on rainbow transfer paper

I love painting background colours. I know though that many people do not have the appropriate equipment or confidence to paint their own fabrics. For some of the projects in this book I have used an iron-on Rainbow transfer paper. This paper has the colours of the rainbow impregnated into it. It is ironed, coloured side down, onto to the right side of the fabric to transfer the colour. This is by far the easiest method to colour fabric and it looks terrific! The colours transfer to the fabric in delicate hues and give added life to some of the plainer cream and white fabrics often used for embroidery.

Another idea is to tear the paper into small pieces and scatter them onto the fabric, especially in and around the outside edges of a floral design, to add interest and shadow effects.

The depth of colour varies with the type of fabric you are using, but is enhanced on polyester-based fabrics. Also, the hotter the iron, the brighter and darker the colours. Due care needs to be given to prevent scorching of the fabric. The photograph gives some indication of the variability.

The transfer paper ironed onto a shiny polyester fabric leaves a very bright image. On polyester/viscose and polyester/cotton (weaver's cloth) mixes, and calico (100% cotton), the colour is not so vibrant and very delicate hues can be achieved for all three fabric types.

The colour from the transfer paper is wash-fast and seems to be permanent. However, it is worthwhile to do a wash test on a selected fabric before going to great efforts on the embroidery. Some fabrics might not hold the colours as well as others.

transfer paper

Iron-on Rainbow transfer paper creates different effects, as shown on these four fabric types

American weaver's cloth

polyester/viscose and flax

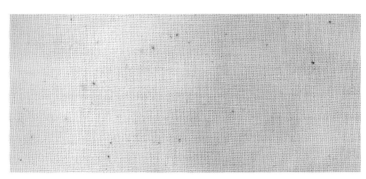

calico (muslin)

100% polyester

Caring for your embroidery

Washing

Punchneedle embroidery worked with traditional punchneedle embroidery in acrylic yarn and embroidery cotton launders very well. Some types of threads do not have the same qualities as cotton or yarn and therefore other factors need to be considered when washing. Punchneedle embroidery was traditionally worked with the loops close together and rather close to the fabric, as in the project Butterflies. This form of punchneedle embroidery washes very well and actually improves with the washing. Often times the embroidery far outlasts the garment it is attached to. Due care is required when washing, to ensure the finished piece doesn't come into contact with Velcro or sharp fasteners which may catch on the loops. Embroideries worked with larger loops and other threads might best be washed gently by hand, just as one washes other sensitive garments or fabrics.

Many of my pieces incorporate reverse punchneedle embroidery (see Stitch Glossary) which is not densely punched, and the stitching is not close together. Careful washing of these pieces is necessary as the stitching may begin to come undone. If I know I will be washing a piece with reverse punchneedle embroidery on it, such as the Cream on Cream cushion, I will sparingly smear the loops on the back with You Can Wash It craft glue which remains soft and pliable. When the glue dries it will hold the rows of loops on the back of the piece in place, and is added insurance against any damage or pulled stitches.

Pressing

I choose not to iron over my embroidery. If the need arises to do so, place the embroidery face down on to a thick, fluffy towel and press into the pile of the towel. Alternatively, use a steam iron in the same manner as working with velvet, holding the iron above the piece and allowing the steam to rise up the pile.

It may be necessary to steam press the fabric around the actual embroidery to remove the mark made by the hoop. This is a good reason to get into the habit of using a doughnut. (See Hoop Techniques.)

5 Threads and ribbons

The thing I love about punchneedle embroidery is the variety of effects created by using many different thicknesses, textures and colours of threads which are readily available in craft shops. As the popular saying goes, 'Colour is music for the eyes.'

A vast range of threads and ribbons—almost anything which can be threaded through the eye of a punchneedle and will flow smoothly through it—can be used for punchneedle embroidery. Very often, if there is any trouble with the thread flowing, all that is needed to fix the problem is simply to choose either a larger needle or a finer thread. Equally, a sign that the thread may be too thick for your needle is when the loops you are working do not stay in place in the fabric you are punching through.

The thread can sometimes be too fine for the punchneedle. This is the case if the fine thread, generally a single strand of thread, seems to 'fall' through the needle in a rush, leaving a loop where the needle penetrates the fabric. If this happens, go to a needle with a smaller bore size, or you may be able to add some tension by gently holding back the thread at the handle end of the punchneedle as you work. Increasing the tension of the fabric in the hoop by pushing up from underneath with your fingers helps as well. Often it is a case of experimenting and trying different combinations of threads and needles to discover what works best and, if there are any limitations what they are.

From one strand of thread up to six strands, 2 mm to 4 mm silk ribbon, some tapestry wools and crewel wool, Bunka thread, crochet cotton, candlewick thread, machine embroidery threads and various exotic threads can be worked through an appropriate sized punchneedle. The thread thickness that can be used is determined by the bore (inside diameter) of the punchneedle—the only requirement is that the thread must flow through the needle smoothly and evenly.

For the projects in this book I have used many types of threads as I enjoy the effects and variety that can be achieved. I use different types of punchneedles for different projects and I know that some threads and ribbons work well in some needles and not in others. You will need to experiment with your own punchneedles and learn their limitations and capabilities. This is part of the fun and magic of punchneedle embroidery!

The threads used in these projects have been chosen because they are generally readily available. You can substitute other threads if a particular one is not easy to find—always remembering the rule, of course, that if a thread type does not flow through your punchneedle, change it. When you substitute threads, the finished piece can look totally different, but in its own right you will have achieved a highly original masterpiece and that, after all, is what embroidery is about.

Acrylic yarn

Acrylic yarn, referred to as Traditional Punchneedle Embroidery acrylic yarn, is used widely for traditional punchneedle embroidery. These yarns, although sold under a number of different brand names, are all very similar.

Acrylic yarn has many really good and valuable qualities. It flows freely through the punchneedle and stays easily in the fabric, owing to the fact that the filaments which constitute the yarn clutch in on themselves. It works up quickly and gives a wonderful full effect, very similar to the effect achieved by using crewel wool. Acrylic yarn is available on a large spool from which it may be directly worked. This is a great timesaver as it is not necessary to re-thread the needle so often. Worked with stitches very close together, acrylic yarn embroidery becomes durable and very washable. Again this is due to the fibres intermingling with each other. After washing the fibres matt together and it becomes near impossible to undo any of the stitching. It can also be brushed, fluffed and sculpted.

I have found that these yarns work up quite differently to a cotton or silk thread when embroidered with a punchneedle. The main difference between acrylic yarn and embroidery cotton, using the same sized punchneedle and the same needle length, is that the size of the formed loops with the acrylic yarn is shorter than with embroidery cotton. Why is this so? I believe it is because the acrylic yarn is made up of small fibres or filaments, which makes it embroider a little like fine wool—the fibres within the yarn cling to each other and also to the fabric when the punchneedle penetrates it, thus not so much thread goes through the fabric resulting in a shorter loop. Cotton or silk threads, being smoother, flow more easily through the needle and work more effortlessly through the fabric. When working acrylic yarn in designs developed for other threads it may be helpful to increase the needle length to give a longer loop.

The acrylic yarn equates in bulk to approximately six strands of Madeira, DMC or other embroidery cottons. One thickness of acrylic yarn works well through the medium punchneedle, as do six strands of embroidery cotton. Use the large punchneedle for 2 thicknesses of acrylic yarn.

While vibrant and interesting colours are available in acrylic yarns, the colour range is limited when compared to embroidery cotton. This makes for some difficulties in directly matching colours from the cotton and silk ranges to acrylic yarn for specific designs. I have recommended highly suitable acrylic yarn colours to replace Madeira or DMC cotton threads in certain projects. It is important to know that if traditional punchneedle embroidery acrylic yarn is not available, then any six-stranded embroidery cotton will be a suitable substitute, or a fine wool such as crewel embroidery wool.

Blending colours with acrylic yarns is difficult as there is no gentle gradation of colours in these ranges.

A finished piece of acrylic yarn embroidery may be ironed over the back with a warm iron. This also assists in matting up the fibres of the yarn, thereby making it near impossible for the stitching to come undone.

Loose filaments of the yarn may rest on the finished embroidery or be stuck on the fabric. A handy way to remove these filaments is by using sticky-tape— pat the sticky side of the tape gently over the embroidery to pick them up.

Embroidery cotton (embroidery floss)

There are many brands of embroidery cotton. It is my understanding that what we know as embroidery cotton in Australia is known as embroidery floss in other countries. What I refer to as embroidery cotton is a thread made up from six separate strands. This can be pulled apart, and from one strand through to six strands can be used effectively for punchneedle embroidery. Different brands of embroidery cotton have different characteristics. My preference is Madeira embroidery cotton, used in many of the projects in the book, but many others also work well. Cross-reference colour charts from Madeira to DMC are available from thread distributors and some craft shops.

Rajmahal art silk

This is a viscose thread with similar properties to some rayon threads. It is made up of six strands which can be separated; from two strands through to all six can be used, depending on the bore of the punchneedle. Stunning results can be achieved: Rajmahal is a thread with a 'wow!' factor. It has a wonderful lustre and comes in a wide range of beautiful colours.

For the punchneedle embroiderer, Rajmahal offers one minor challenge. It is shiny and slippery and the starting and finishing threads often slip through to the front of the fabric. There are a couple of ways around this. Firstly, when the punchneedle is threaded, tie a small knot in the end of the thread. This at least holds some ends in place. Secondly, smearing a little washable craft glue on the trimmed ends as each section is finished is worth considering. Method: squeeze a very tiny amount of glue onto a small piece of paper. Dip a pin in the glue and smear a small amount onto the end thread. When dry this will hold the first and last stitches neatly in place.

It is worthwhile going to this extra effort and thereby gaining stunning results from the use of Rajmahal art silks.

Silk ribbons

The ribbons of interest to a punchneedle embroider will be either 2 mm or 4 mm silk ribbons. They can be in plain colours or hand-dyed, in any of the many brands available from specialist embroidery and craft shops. Silk ribbons are usually much

TIP

You cannot compare two pieces of embroidery, one done with acrylic yarn and the other with embroidery cotton or silk thread, as they are so vastly different. View each piece alone; one without the other, and as an individual piece. Each looks just gorgeous! An example of this is the Wicker Basket.

I have touched on only a few types of threads, those which I have used in this book. There is an abundance of threads. Head off to your nearest craft store or use the Internet to find out what is available. With punchneedle embroidery give anything a go!! Remember: if the chosen thread has difficulty flowing through the punchneedle or it flows through too quickly and without control, *chances are it is the thread* that is the problem, not the punchneedle. Simply change the thread or change the size of the punchneedle!

softer than the polyester ribbons so widely available and the thickness of the polyester ribbons mean they may not be easily threaded through the punchneedle. It is therefore important to use a very soft ribbon and to test the threading and its flow through your punchneedle. See Working with Silk Ribbon (page 26) and the Ribbon Heart project.

A special punchneedle is available for use with wide ribbons; this is the Dancing Ribbon needle which very easily and beautifully embroiders 7 mm (¼ in) and 13 mm (½ in) silk ribbon. See A Promise of Summer.

1 SCISSORS CASE BEAUTY

A beautiful hand-embroidered scissors case for one of the most cherished tools of the embroiderer. It is a lovely thing to have and to use, and a precious handmade gift to give. The case on the left is worked in Madeira embroidery cotton, the case on the right in Cameo acrylic yarn.

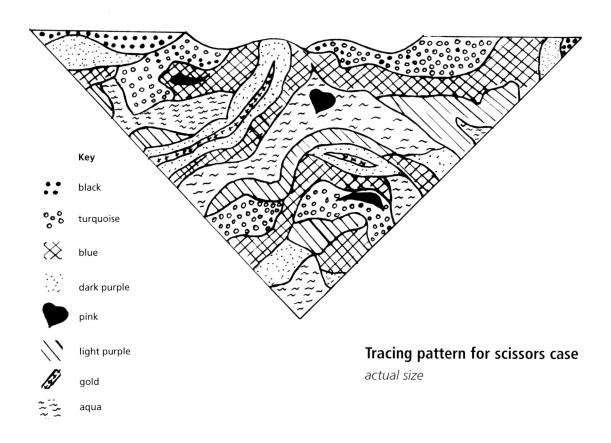

Key

• • black

∘ turquoise

✕ blue

∴ dark purple

♥ pink

⟍⟍ light purple

gold

~~ aqua

Tracing pattern for scissors case
actual size

Materials

20 cm (8 in) lip-lock hoop
25 cm (10 in) square of fabric
fabric for lining
sharp embroidery scissors
medium punchneedle (for acrylic yarn)
small punchneedle (for embroidery cotton)
sewing needle and thread
You Can Wash It Craft glue

Threads

Embroidery cotton

Madeira	DMC
black	black
dark purple 903	dark purple 333
light purple 804	light purple 208
blue 1006	blue 798
aqua 1108	aqua 3810
pink 706	pink 917
turquoise 2507	turquoise 3808
gold metallic 5014	gold metallic

Traditional punchneedle embroidery acrylic yarn

The colour conversion from one acrylic yarn to another is not always exact. Where a colour is not an absolute match I have chosen colours that work well together.

Cameo	Pretty Punch
dark lavender 37	*grape 7*
light lavender 36	*dark lavender 8*
blue 74	*bright blue 51*
teal 50	*jade 47*

fuchsia 80	*neon 2*
deep turquoise 83	*peacock 74*
metallic copper/silver/lavender 602	*gold MG*
black	*black*

Preparation

Trace the design onto the back of fabric. Place the fabric in the hoop with the traced design uppermost, ensuring that it is extremely tight in the hoop.

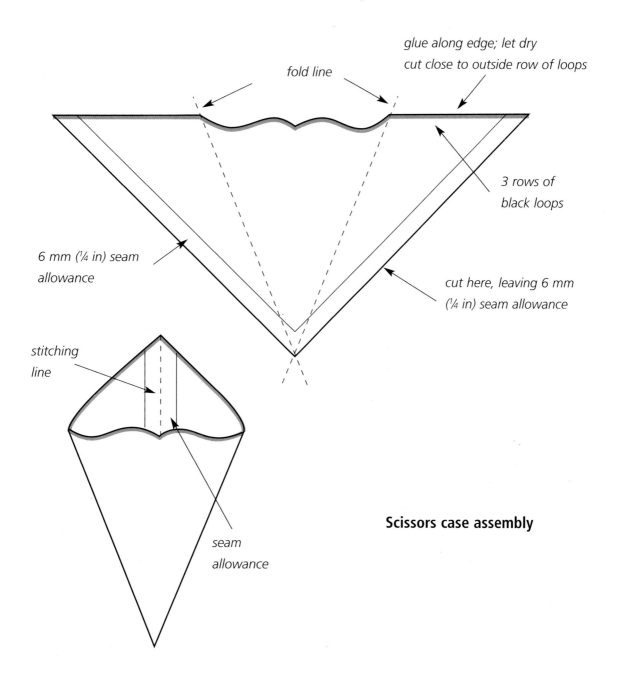

glue along edge; let dry
cut close to outside row of loops

fold line

*3 rows of
black loops*

*6 mm (¼ in) seam
allowance*

*cut here, leaving 6 mm
(¼ in) seam allowance*

*stitching
line*

*seam
allowance*

Scissors case assembly

69

Embroidery

Determine where the different coloured threads are to be used. Use either three strands of embroidery cotton in the small punchneedle or a single thickness of acrylic yarn in the medium punchneedle.

Set the punchneedle at No 1.

Embroider the black outlines of the shapes with 1 row of stitching, placing the stitches very close together. It is not necessary to outline the pink and metallic thread areas.

Work 3 rows of black along the top of the design, taking particular care to work the stitches on the very outside row really close together.

Fill in the blocks of colour, leaving the equivalent of 1 row of stitching unworked next to each row of black stitches. Leaving this small space prevents the different coloured loops becoming intermingled, and helps define each area. Work the stitches very closely together along the outside straight edges.

Keep the back free from long ends of thread which can accidentally get pulled.

Finishing

Remove the fabric from the hoop and stretch it in all directions to straighten the embroidery.

Glue lightly over the back of the finished piece, giving good coverage to the top edge. Allow the glue to dry.

Carefully cut along the loops on the top edge.

Cut along the straight sides, leaving a 6 mm (¼ in) seam allowance along both.

Bringing the straight sides together, form the piece into a cone shape with the patterned looped surface on the outside. Tuck in the seam allowance, matching the coloured areas on each side and in particular trying to match up the black lines. The aim is to end up with an almost invisible seam. It is helpful to trim away some of the seam allowance at the very point of the scissors case to minimise bulk in that area.

Using a strong thread, start stitching about 3 cm (1 ¼ in) up from the point, working down to the point. Take a small stitch on one side, directly at the base of the loops. Put the needle into the fabric on the other side, immediately across from where the first stitch came out, at the very base of the loops. Take a small stitch sideways and repeat.

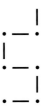

**Stitch movement used
in joining back of case**

Pull the stitches firmly together. The loops will join up to cover the seam line. At the very tip stitching can become a little difficult. Once you get to the tip, pull the stitching very firmly again and then finish off.

There may be some tiny areas of fabric showing between the loops of embroidery. If this happens, take a sewing needle with thread the same colour as the loops and stitch in some loops to cover any visible fabric.

Go back to where you started and work up to the top in the same manner to complete the seam.

Lining

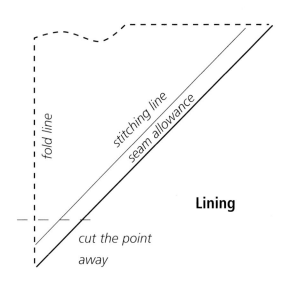

Trace the case pattern onto the lining fabric and place the fabric tightly in the hoop. With black cotton or yarn, embroider one row of loops along the top edge, very close together, with the needle set at No 2.

Remove from the hoop. Glue along the top edge. Allow to dry.

Cut the lining out, leaving a 6 mm (¼ in) seam allowance on the straight sides, and cut along the glued loops at the top. With the right sides of the fabric together stitch along the seam allowance.

Remove the point from the lining by cutting off 2 cm (¾ in), which eliminates extra bulk, and then finish the cut edge neatly.

Finger press the seam allowance open. Place the lining inside the case. Gently flatten the case into shape by hand.

With black thread, stitch together the loops at the top of the case and the lining.

Optional Finish the top of the case by attaching a length of braid. See Braid making at the end of the Stitch Glossary.

2 OVERFLOWING CORNUCOPIA

With pretty feet and pretty braids, this little cushioned stool overflowing with
perfumed flowers is a joy to behold. The embroidery is worked in the vibrant colours
of Rajmahal art silks.

Stitch guide

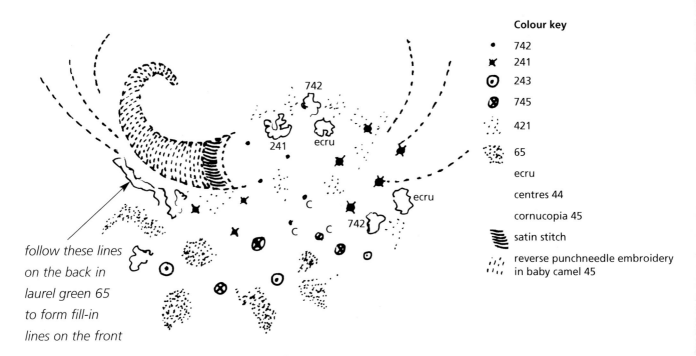

Colour key

•	742
✖	241
◉	243
✪	745
⋮	421
⣿	65
	ecru
	centres 44
	cornucopia 45
≋	satin stitch
⫶⫶	reverse punchneedle embroidery in baby camel 45

742

241   ecru

ecru

C

C   C   742

C

*follow these lines
on the back in
laurel green 65
to form fill-in
lines on the front*

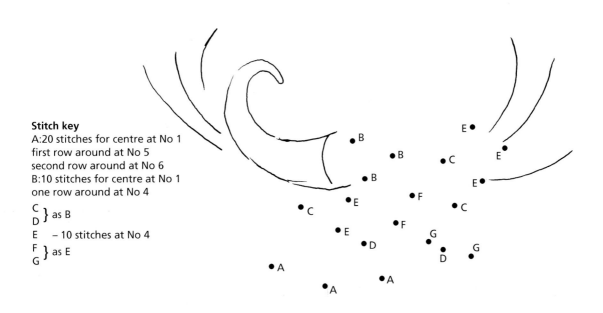

Stitch key
A:20 stitches for centre at No 1
first row around at No 5
second row around at No 6
B:10 stitches for centre at No 1
one row around at No 4

C
D } as B

E – 10 stitches at No 4

F
G } as E

E
B
B
C
E
B
E
C
E
F
C
E
F
D
G
A
D
G
A
A

Tracing pattern for Overflowing Cornucopia

actual size

Materials

20 cm (8 in) lip-lock hoop
30 cm (12 in) square fabric
sharp embroidery scissors
medium punchneedle
white or coloured dressmaker's carbon
sewing needle and strong thread
round wooden stool with little legs, approx.
    13 cm (5 ½ inches) diameter

Threads

Rajmahal Art Silk
damask rose 742
dusty rose 241
grape 243
bordeaux 745
green earth 421
laurel green 65
tangier gold 44
baby camel 45
ecru

Preparation

Normally I recommend that a design is not traced onto the cross or bias of the fabric. This is particularly so for framed pieces of work. If, however, you intend to cover a round or otherwise curved object, it is very much easier to stretch the fabric over such a shape if you are using the bias. So, this is one rare instance when I suggest for ease of finishing the piece that the design is traced and worked on the bias.

Measure the top of the wooden stool and mark this shape onto the fabric, leaving sufficient allowance to secure the fabric under the item.

Centre the tracing on the fabric. Trace the outline of the cornucopia and the extended lines shown on the pattern onto the front of the fabric. Trace the dots for the flowers and areas of greenery onto the back of the fabric.

Place the fabric tightly in the hoop with the tracing of the cornucopia uppermost.

Embroidery

Following the stitch guide, work the cornucopia in reverse punchneedle embroidery with baby camel 45. (See figure 3, sample b, in the Stitch Glossary.)

Working in this manner gives a lovely effect to the 'horn of plenty'. The area near the mouth of the cornucopia is embroidered in satin stitch (see Stitch Glossary, figure 7, h and i).

Work the green lines in green earth 421 with reverse punchneedle embroidery.

Remove the fabric from the hoop, turn it over and replace it tightly in the hoop with the back of the design facing uppermost.

Follow the instructions on the pattern for working the flowers and greenery. Each flower is coded for the colours and stitches required, beginning ecru in the centres of the A and B flowers. (Refresh your memory of how to create flowers by referring back to figure 6 in the Stitch Glossary.)

Assembling embroidery: cut around shape, work running stitch along stitch line, and pull ends of thread to tighten

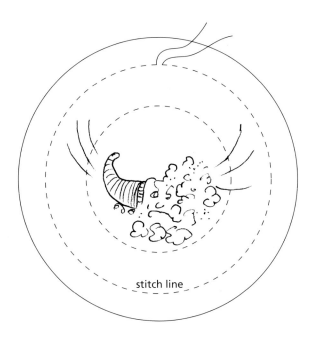

stitch line

Embroider the green in and around the flowers with loops made with the needle set at No 1. The darker green laurel 65 is indicated on the pattern by the more heavily dotted areas. The more lightly dotted areas indicate green earth 421.

Finishing

Trim any long ends from the back, remove the work from the hoop, and press around the embroidery.

Cut pellon or wadding to fit over the shape you are using.

Cut around the embroidery, leaving sufficient fabric to turn under.

With a sewing needle and strong thread, place a line of running stitches around the seam allowance. Centre the fabric over the pellon on the stool. Pull the running stitches tight and secure the ends of the sewing thread.

Assemble the embroidered top and the legs of the stool together.

Take one thickness of each Rajmahal colour used in the embroidery to make a braid (see Braid Making in the Stitch Glossary), and stitch or glue the braid in place.

3 BUTTERFLIES

*Add the charm and grace to towels, other manchester and soft furnishings that only
a butterfly can bring. These lovely butterflies on the handtowel and face cloth have
been embroidered and then appliquéd. Punchneedle embroidery does not work so well
on towelling as the loops tend to get a bit lost, but I find that appliquéd
designs on towels and face cloths launder and last very well.
The butterflies are worked in embroidery cotton.*

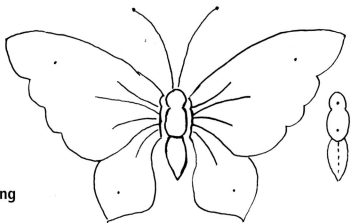

Tracing pattern and blending guide for large butterfly

Blending 6 strands of thread

6A	4A 2B	4B 2A	6B	4B 2C	4C 2B	6C

A = 604 dark pink
B = 605 medium pink
C = 606 light pink

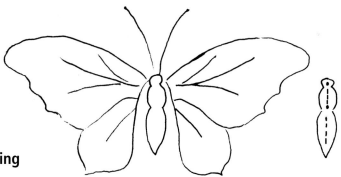

Tracing pattern and blending guide for small butterfly

Blending 3 strands of thread

3A	2A 1B	2B 1A	3B	2B 1C	2C 1B	3C

A = 604 dark pink
B = 605 medium pink
C = 606 light pink

Materials

small and medium punchneedles

20 cm (8 in) lip-lock hoop

25 cm (10 in) square of tightly woven fabric

You Can Wash It craft glue

fine lead pencil or iron-on heat-transfer pen

sharp embroidery scissors

fine steel crochet hook

TIP

You will notice that there is a space on the design between the wings and body. The body is worked with the punchneedle set at Nos 3 and 4 which makes the loops longer. The longer the loops, the more area they cover. Without the unworked space, the body will become indistinguishable from the wings.

Embroidery cottons

The larger butterfly on the hand towel has been worked with six strands of embroidery cotton in a medium punchneedle. The smaller butterfly on the face cloth has been worked with three strands of embroidery cotton in a small punchneedle.

Madeira	DMC
dark pink 604	*dark pink 3687*
medium pink 605	*medium pink 3688*
light pink 606	*light pink 3716*

Preparation

Trace the design onto the back of the fabric using your preferred method—either a lead pencil or a heat-transfer pen. Place the fabric in the hoop with the traced design uppermost. Ensure that the fabric is extremely taut in the hoop and the hoop nut is done up really tight.

These butterflies have been worked using the Blending technique (see Stitch Glossary, figure 17) with Madeira threads. Substitute colour numbers if using DMC threads.

Large butterfly

Six strands of thread are used in medium punchneedle set at No 1.

Wings Outline all the veins on the wings with 1 row of stitching, using dark pink 604.

Follow the chart with the pattern which indicates how many strands of each colour to use to fill in the wings. For example: 4A/2B means that you take four strands of colour A (604), put them with two strands of colour B (605) and thread all six strands through the needle, using them all together.

Working inwards, blend the colours for the fill-in rows until there is no remaining space. Work only 1 row with each colour change. Work around the dark lines of the veins. If there is a small area left to fill in when all the colour changes have been completed, fill it in with pale pink.

The four tiny dots, each consisting of a single stitch in dark pink 604, are put in at the completion of the embroidery (see figure 19, Stitch Glossary). On the back of the embroidery mark where the dots are to be placed. With the punchneedle set at No 2, gently guide the needle through the embroidery, taking care not to push out any of the already formed loops. If the dots are sitting too high, take the tags on the back of the fabric and gently pull them until the loop forming the dot is at the same level as the remaining embroidery.

Head and body The head is worked at No 3 with 12 stitches in a circle in dark pink. Use the dot on the pattern as the centre starting point. See figure 6, Stitch Glossary.

The thorax is worked at No 4 with 12 stitches in a circle in medium pink

The abdomen is worked in pale pink at No 3 with 5 stitches straight down. Work all the way around these stitches at No 2, and then all the way around at No 1.

Small butterfly

Wings Three strands of thread are used in a small punchneedle set at No 1.

Outline the veins on the wings with 1 row of dark pink 604.

Follow the chart with the pattern indicating how many strands of each colour to use to fill in the wings. For example: 2A/1B means that you take two strands of colour A (604), put them with one strand of colour B (605) and thread all three strands through the needle, using them together.

The outlines of the wings are worked with 2 rows of dark pink.

On the top wings, working inwards, work 2 rows for each colour change. Depending on how closely the stitching has been worked, there may not be space to work the last pale pink colour change. This is of no great concern.

The bottom wings have only 1 row worked with each colour change.

Head and body The head is worked at No 1 with 8 stitches in a circle in dark pink (see figure 6, Stitch Glossary).

The thorax is worked with 3 stitches straight down at No 3 in medium pink, than at No 2 all the way around, then No 1 all the way around.

The abdomen is worked in pale pink with 4 stitches straight down at No 2, then the shape is filled in at No 1.

Finishing

Remove the fabric from the hoop and stretch it in all directions to straighten out the butterflies.

Glue around the outside edge of the completed embroidery on the back of the work, also gluing the spaces between the wings and the bodies. Do not glue over the entire back of the butterflies at this stage—they will be glued all over when you stick them to the towel, and two layers of glue can make the butterflies feel too hard.

Allow the glue to dry.

Cut each butterfly away from the fabric. Although from the back it appears that the body is not joined to the wings, leave most of the fabric between the body and the wings as a bridge to hold the butterfly together, otherwise the design will fall to pieces. Check from the front of the embroidery to see how much joining fabric can be cut away.

Make hand-twisted braids for the antennae using two strands each of the three pinks (see Braid Making in Stitch Glossary). For the larger butterfly make the finished braid 70 mm (2 ¾ in) long, for the smaller butterfly 50 mm (2 in). At each of the very ends of the braid tie a double knot. Give the knots a gentle tug to check they are secure, then trim the ends close to the knots.

Fold the antennae in half and glue the fold under the head on the back of the embroidery. Glue all over the back of the butterflies and then position them in place on the towels. Leave to dry.

With a sewing needle and a small sewing stitch, couch the antennae into place or use a very fine line of glue to stick them down.

These beautifully decorated towels will be received with absolute pleasure when given as a gift.

4 DANDY BEAR

*Rugged up in his winter woollies, this dandy bear will look equally wonderful
attached to a favourite jumper or happily looking out from a frame.
The embroidery on the jumper is worked in traditional punchneedle embroidery
acrylic yarn. The framed bear is worked with three strands of embroidery cotton.*

Tracing pattern for Dandy Bear
actual size

Materials

20 cm (8 in) lip-lock hoop

25 cm (10 in) square fabric

sharp embroidery scissors

medium and small punchneedles

iron-on heat-transfer pen

sewing needle

fine crochet hook

Threads

Embroidery cottons

Madeira	DMC
light brown 2103	light brown 3828
white 2402	white
blue 1006	blue 336
dark blue 1007	dark blue 517
grey 1801	grey 414
rusty orange 214	rusty orange 351
black 2400	black 310

Traditional punchneedle embroidery acrylic yarn

The colour conversion from one acrylic yarn to another is not always exact. Where a colour is not an absolute match I have chosen colours that work well together.

Cameo	Pretty Punch
taupe 59	medium sand 33
white	white
deep copen 9	marine 76
blue navy 13	use black
dark grey 66	charcoal grey 59
burnt orange 73	watermelon 1
black	black

Use the small punchneedle with three strands of embroidery cotton.

For the acrylic yarns, work with the medium punchneedle.

Preparation

Read about stretching fabric in the Fabric section. Trace the design onto the back of your chosen fabric. Assemble the fabric tightly into the hoop.

These instructions refer to Madeira colours. Substitute colours if using other threads or yarns.

Head

I suggest you work the bear's head first. It is nice to know that the facial features look good before proceeding with the rest of the embroidery. It can be a great disappointment to put in a lot of work on the body and then find out that you are unable to get the face looking great.

At this stage, leave the inside areas indicated by dotted lines around the eyes and ears on the pattern unworked.

With light brown 2103 and punchneedle set at No 4, work 1 row along the dotted line shown on the pattern from the forehead to between the eyes.

Work 4 rows on either side of the dotted line at No 4.

Work 4 rows at No 3 on either side of the previous 4 rows.

Work 4 rows at No 2 on either side of the previous 4 rows.

Work remaining area of the head at No 1. There is a larger area to work at No 1 on one side.

Work 3 rows at No 1 under the nose in the chin area.

At this stage, leave the area under the eyes unworked (see diagram 1).

Work at No 1 all the way around the head area with the stitches very close together to neaten the edge.

Diagram 1

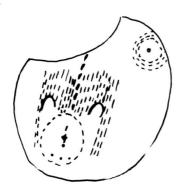

Ears Work at No 7 with 25 stitches in a circle, starting in the centre (see Stitch Glossary, figure 6).

Diagram 2

Nose Set punchneedle at No 12 and work 3 stitches in a line (see diagram 2). Work around these 3 stitches with 1 row at No 11, 1 row at No 10, 1 row at No 9 and 1 row at No 8.

Now with sharp scissors cut and shape the loops on the ears and the nose. Although it is often easier to trim and shape when the fabric has been removed from the hoop, this is not necessary for such a small area. If this is the first time you have done any shaping, trim the nose gently and continue to trim until you are satisfied with the shape. If you are not happy after the shaping has been done, go back and punch in some more loops and start over again. Refer to the photograph of the finished bear for guidance.

Black area of nose Mark a dot on the back of the fabric where the black area will be worked. Set punchneedle at No 8 and carefully work 5 stitches as close together as possible. If there has not been sufficient trimming of the nose area, the No 8 black loops might not show through. In that case, trim a little more from the shaped nose. It is difficult to get all of the loops to come together when punching through an area which has already been worked. It might be necessary to gently push the black loops together with the tip of the needle.

Sometimes it seems that no matter how many times you try, the black part of the nose area just doesn't turn out the way you want it to. There is an alternative method. Take 50 cm (20 in) of six strands of black cotton. Fold in four. Tie a knot by wrapping the thread around twice and work it into the centre of the thread (see diagram 3).

Diagram 3: Tying a knot is an alternative method of making a nose

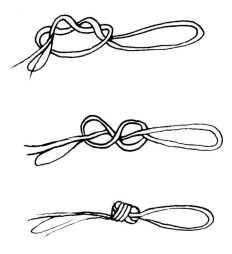

At each side of the dot marked for the black area, gently make an opening between the fibres of the fabric with a crochet hook. Pull an end of the black thread through each opening from the front to the back (or thread the two ends of the made knot through a sewing needle and stitch from the front to the back). Position the knot in place on the front. Tie the ends at the back to secure the knot or secure the untied ends with a smear of glue.

Black lines The black line from the nose to the mouth, and the line for the mouth, are worked from the front. Set the punchneeedle at No 7 and work the vertical line from the nose to the mouth by punching on the two dots indicated on the pattern (see diagram 4)—this creates a long black stitch on the front overlaying the furry nose. Pull the beginning and end tags through to the back.

Tie the threads together, leaving enough slack on the front so that the black line just rests upon the fur. Work the horizontal line for the mouth in the same manner.

If you have difficulty getting a pleasing effect this way, take a sewing needle threaded with black thread and hand-embroider the lines into the marked areas.

Diagram 4

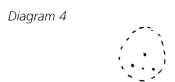

Eyes With black, work at No 3 with 10 stitches around in a circle. With white, work 5 or 6 stitches very close together, only on the dots shown on the side of the black circle (see diagram 5).

Diagram 5

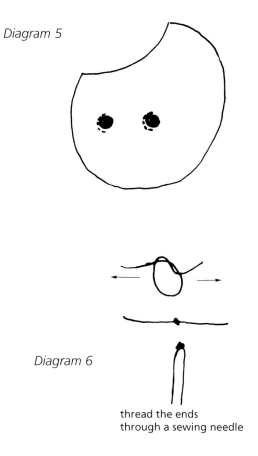

Diagram 6

thread the ends through a sewing needle

A small white dot needs to be worked in each eye at the position 11 o'clock. This is difficult to place in just the right spot with the punchneedle, so use the knot method. Take three strands of white cotton 10 cm (4 in) in length. Tie a knot into the centre of the length (see diagram 6). Fold the thread in half and position the knot at the looped end. Thread the two cut ends through a sewing needle and, from the front of the work, make a stitch to the back. Pull the ends at the back to seat the knot position on the front of the eye. Repeat for the second eye. Tie the ends together at the back, or secure the untied ends with a smear of glue.

Hat

Crown With black, and punchneedle set at No 3, work 1 row along dotted line marked on the pattern.

Work 4 rows on either side of dotted line at No 3.

Work 4 rows at No 2 on either side of the previous 4 rows.

Work the remainder at No 1.

Work 1 row all the way around the hat at No 1 with the stitches very close together to neaten the edge.

Brim Still using black, follow diagram 7, working 3 rows at No 4, and 2 rows at No 3 where indicated. The remainder is worked at No 2.

Diagram 7

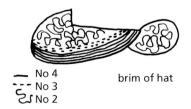

—— No 4
---- No 3
ᒫᒣ No 2

brim of hat

Work 1 row all the way around the brim at No 1, with the stitches very close together, to neaten the edge. Working in this manner by changing the length of the needle tip gives added dimension to the embroidery.

Hatband Work with rusty orange 214 at No 2.

Vest

Stitch the pocket line with 2 rows at No 5 with the darker blue 1007. The remainder of the vest is worked in blue 1006 with the punchneedle set at No 4, leaving a one-row space between the scarf outline and the two parts of the vest.

Scarf

Worked in white, leaving a one-row space between the head and the first row of the scarf under the neck area.

Work the first row under the neck at No 1, second row at No 2, third row at No 3, fourth row at No 4, fifth row at No 5 and the remaining area at No 5 (see diagram 8).

Diagram 8

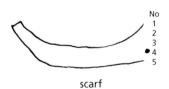

No
1
2
3
4
5

scarf

Knot Work the knot of the scarf on the dot marked, at No 12 with 20 stitches in a circle.

Long end of the scarf Work 1 row very close together around the edges at No 1. Fill in with No 5.

Fringe Remove the outside casing from the punchneedle, which gives a much longer length to the needle tip, and work 2 rows across the bottom of the scarf. Cut the loops open and trim the fringe to straighten it.

Pullover

Worked in rusty orange 214, leaving a one-row space away from the vest, and a space approximately 4 rows wide directly under the fringe of the scarf. This allows the fringe to sit flatter.

Work the pullover at No 2. Work 1 row all the way around each outside edge of the arms at No 1 with the stitches very close together to neaten the edge.

Trousers

Worked in blue 1006 and grey 1801 stripes (see figure 13, Stitch Glossary).

Work at No 1. Only one line is drawn on the pattern to indicate the stripes. Work along this line with 2 rows of blue and then work next to this with 2 rows of grey, leaving almost a row's width between each colour. Continue alternating the colours until the whole trouser area is filled in.

Work 1 row all the way around the edges at No 1, matching the colours of the stripes, with the stitches very close together.

Shoes

Worked in black with soles in grey 1801. The soles are worked first at No 1.

The lines of the laces are worked in rusty orange 214 at No 3, with 2 rows close together. Work this colour before the black, which is then worked at No 2.

To make the bows for the laces, thread a sewing needle with a length of rusty orange 214, double the thread and tie a knot. Stitch the thread through from the back, cut the needle off the thread on the front and tie a bow at the top of the shoe. Trim the ends.

Finishing

This delightful bear can be framed, or worked in the appliqué method (see page 59) and put on a baby blanket, jumper or sweat shirt.

Whatever you do with him, he will look fabulous in any application and everyone will want to know: 'How did you do it?'

5 DELIGHTFUL DAISIES

A very simple but stunning design. The delightful daisies sit very prettily on a spectacles case. The orange daisies on the black and white case are worked in Madeira stranded embroidery cotton, the white daisies on the red and green case in traditional punchneedle embroidery acrylic yarn.

Threads

Madeira embroidery cotton	Cameo acrylic	Pretty Punch acrylic
dark green 1504	dark aspen 26	dark aspen 68
light green 1502	aspen green 25	aspen green 67
yellow 113	gold yellow 45	bright lemon 55
orange 206	white	white

The conversion from one acrylic yarn to the other is not always exact. Where a colour is not an absolute match I have chosen colours that work well together.

Tracing pattern for Delightful Daisies

actual size

Materials

20 cm (8 in) lip-lock hoop
25 cm (10 in) square fabric
sharp embroidery scissors
small punchneedle
iron-on interfacing (optional)
fabric for lining
ladybird charm

This is the drawing from which the daisy tracing pattern was made. Notice how much has been eliminated from this drawing. Having less detail in the final design reduces the denseness of the embroidery.

To understand how necessary it is to minimise the amount of detail put into a drawing that you are taking from a design source, compare the original drawing of the daisies with the tracing pattern. If the initial drawing was used as the tracing pattern there will be very little distinction between the petals so that when the flowers are completely embroidered they would look like a blob!

Preparation

Trace the design onto the back of the fabric. I used some beautiful silk fabrics backed with iron-on woven interfacing.

Place the fabric in the hoop with the tracing uppermost, ensuring that the fabric is extremely tight.

Use the same needle lengths for both cotton and acrylic yarns.

Use three strands of embroidery cotton in the small needle, or a single thickness of acrylic yarn. There is some resistance with the flow of acrylic yarn through the bore of the small needle but I used this to great effect, and achieved a really nice short loop. The acrylic yarn works through the small punchneedle very well—the only place you need to be careful is when cutting the thread. Hold the thread securely at its point of exit from the fabric, otherwise it is very easy to pull undone the last stitch. If you find the acrylic yarn difficult to work through the small punchneedle, change to a medium one.

Centres

With the yellow, work along the dotted line with 5 stitches for the big flower and 3 stitches for the smaller flower with the needle set at No 3. Work all the way around at No 2. Fill in the remaining area with No 1. Changing the length of the needle tip gives a domed effect to the flower centres. (See Stitch Glossary, figure 5, sample c.)

Petals

Work the petals at No 1 in Madeira orange or acrylic white.

The next step is a great trick to know if part of a design has lost definition. Having completed the petals, a row of reverse punchneedle embroidery is worked from the front of the fabric. This tidies up the edges and gives the petals a more defined shape. Work this row by pushing the loops out of the way and punching the stitches into the base of the loops. Pull the beginning and end threads through to the back of the fabric and trim.

Leaves and stem

The leaf is worked at No 1 with the two greens. Work the lines of the veins as one row.

The design worked in acrylic yarn has the vein worked in dark green with the remainder of the leaf in light green.

The orange daisy, which is worked in embroidery cotton, has the leaf vein worked in pale green and the rest of the leaf filled in with dark green.

Embroider the stem in green with the needle set at No 1.

Finishing

Remove embroidery from hoop and stretch fabric in all directions to straighten it.

Make these lovely embroideries into a spectacle case or a pencil case using your preferred method for assembling a soft fabric case. Stitch the ladybird charm to one of the petals.

Another great idea for using these colourful daisies is to work them on teatowels or handtowels. Refer to the Butterflies project for hints on working with towelling.

6 GIRAFFES

These easily embroidered giraffes add charm to
a toddler's shirt and trousers.

Tracing pattern for Giraffes
actual size

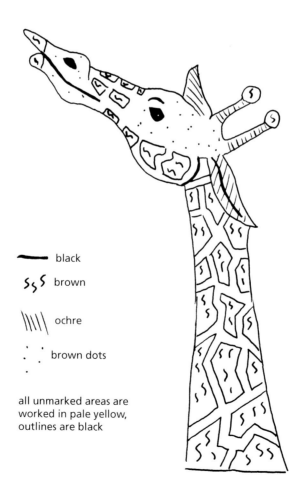

──── black

$\varsigma\varsigma\varsigma$ brown

\\\\\\ ochre

⠂∴ brown dots

all unmarked areas are
worked in pale yellow,
outlines are black

Materials

small punchneedle

15 cm (6 in) lip-lock hoop

22 cm (9 in) square of black fabric

You Can Wash It craft glue

On'N'Off craft glue (optional)

white or coloured dressmaker's carbon

sharp embroidery scissors

fine steel crochet hook

sewing needle

Embroidery cottons

Madeira	DMC
pale yellow 102	pale yellow 3078
dark brown 2005	dark brown 938
ochre 2302	ochre 976
black	black

Preparation

Trace the design onto the back of the fabric using the dressmaker's carbon. Place the fabric in the hoop with the traced design uppermost, ensuring that the fabric is extremely tight.

Three strands are used throughout in the small needle.

Work the giraffes one at a time—only one will fit in the hoop.

TIP

Work outline stitches close together so that there is a solid line of stitching to edge the design.

Embroidery

Set the needle at No 1.

Outline the giraffe in black with the stitches very close together.

The bold lines for the throat, mouth, eyes, eyebrow on the giraffe looking up, the nostrils, and within the ears, are also worked in black, with the stitches close together.

Fill in the dark brown patches, then work the pale yellow areas of the face and between the brown patches.

Change the needle length to No 2 to make the dots on the giraffes' faces in brown, working the dots through the previously embroidered yellow (see figure 19, Stitch Glossary). Work the dots randomly, being guided by the colour photograph and the pattern.

Change the needle tip to No 8 for the mane, working one row very close together with the ochre colour. See the colour photograph for placement. Trim the mane by cutting the loops to about 6 mm (¼ in).

The eyelashes, only worked on the giraffe looking down, are worked last of all. (See closeup of giraffe on shirt pocket.) Set the needle tip to No 7 and carefully work along the upper edge of the eye. Cut and trim the loops to shape.

Put in the white for the eyes, using either of these methods. Change to the medium needle with six strands of thread and carefully punch in 1 loop. Alternatively, take a length of six strands of thread. Tie a knot in the centre. Thread the two ends through a sewing needle, and stich from the front to the back leaving the knot on the top. Secure the ends at the back. (See diagram 6 in the Dandy Bear project.)

Finishing

Remove the completed embroidery from the hoop and stretch the fabric into shape.

Glue all over the back of the design with You Can Wash It craft glue and leave to dry.

These gorgeous giraffes can be glued again with the You Can Wash It craft glue and placed into position on a garment so that they are permanent.

Alternatively, a fun thing to do is to smear the back with the On'N'Off craft glue and put aside until it is 'tacky' dry (this takes 6—8 hours). The giraffe can then be put on and taken off at whim. When not being used, store the giraffe on a sheet of plastic, or on the glass of a small photo frame, and display him in your child's room.

A giraffe with You Can Wash It craft glue smeared all over the back, dried and cut out, can also be made up into a friendly finger puppet for a little one.

7 NASTURTIUMS

Bright, bold and beautiful, this cushion makes a statement. The dramatic black background showcases the vibrant nasturtiums worked in traditional punchneedle embroidery acrylic yarn.

Materials

medium punchneedle
25 cm (10 in) lip-lock hoop
35 cm (14 in) square of tightly woven fabric
sharp embroidery scissors
white or coloured dressmaker's carbon
fine steel crochet hook

Acrylic threads

Cameo	Pretty Punch
lime 28	spring green 3
aspen green 25	aspen green 67
antique gold 47	antique gold 71
gold 46	yellow gold 56
burnt orange 73	orange 40 or 73
blue 74	bright blue 51

The colour conversions are not always exact, but I have chosen colours that work well together.

Preparation

Photocopy the design at 133%, and trace it onto the back of the fabric using the dressmaker's carbon. The white or coloured carbon is easily seen on black fabric.

Place the fabric in the hoop with the traced design uppermost. Ensure that the fabric is extremely tight in the hoop.

Embroidery

These instructions use Cameo colours. Substitute the colours if using Pretty Punch yarns.

The main parts of the design are worked in normal punchneedle embroidery. The placement for overstitching and reverse punchneedle embroidery is indicated on the pattern. See Stitch Glossary, page 28.

Use the medium needle throughout, with the needle set at No 1 except for the centres.

This design is worked leaving areas of black fabric showing through the embroidery. These areas are shaded on the pattern.

Centres

With lime green 28, and the needle set at No 3, work 8 stitches in a circle for flower 1 (see figure 6, Stitch Glossary), and 10 stitches in a circle for flower 2. Change to No 2 and work one row all the way around both centres.

Leaves and calyx

Work at No 1. I chose lime green 28 as the best colour match for nasturtium leaves, but it is a little too bright when used alone. To counteract this, when the leaves and calyx are finished add extra stitching in aspen green 25 among the lime green to soften the brightness. Overpunching with this second green tones down the vibrancy just enough to add a subtle effect to the leaves.

To work the leaves, begin by embroidering the outer lines and fill in all the unshaded areas on the pattern. The shaded areas are not worked at all, allowing the black fabric to show through.

Flowers 1 and 2

Set the punchneedle at No 1 and work the outside lines of the petals, then fill in all the unshaded areas. Petals numbered 1, 2 and 3 are embroidered with gold 46. Petals numbered 4 and 5 are worked with burnt orange 73.

Flower 3

Set the punchneedle at No 1 and work the outside lines of the petals, then fill in all the unshaded areas of the petals, with burnt orange 73.

If there appears to be too much black fabric showing between the petals and leaves, work more rows of colour. If there seems to be insufficient black showing to define each area,

Tracing pattern for Nasturtiums

enlarge at 133%

Key

shaded areas indicate no stitching

overstitching reverse punchneedle embroidery

reverse punchneedle embroidery

especially the markings on the petals, remove some stitches. Use the photograph as a guide.

When all the sections worked in normal punchneedle embroidery are completed, they are outlined from the front with reverse punchneedle embroidery (see figure 14, sample 1, b, Stitch Glossary) to give the leaves and petals a more defined edge.

Stems, tendrils and wavy lines

The stems and tendrils are worked in antique gold 47, using both reverse overstitching (figure 7, sample d, Stitch Glossary) and reverse punchneedle embroidery as shown on the pattern. It will be necessary to move the hoop over some of the completed areas of embroidery. Use a doughnut (see Hoop Techniques) to protect the work.

To complete the design, stitch the wavy lines in blue 74 in reverse punchneedle embroidery.

Finishing

Trim the ends on the back. Remove the fabric from the hoop and stretch it in all directions to straighten the embroidery. As a precaution, to prevent any ends coming loose behind the reverse punchneedle embroidery of the stems and blue lines, smear a little You Can Wash It craft glue on the thread ends on the back of the piece.

Make this colourful design into a cushion using your preferred method for assembling a cushion.

These colourful nasturtiums will also look gorgeous in a frame.

8 CHRISTMAS DECORATIONS

Add bright colour around the house at Christmas with these very easily embroidered decorations. Hang them from the tree, frame them or give as a heartfelt gift. They are worked in traditional punchneedle embroidery acrylic yarn and six strands of embroidery cotton.

Christmas Decorations worked with traditional punchneedle embroidery acrylic yarn.

Materials

medium punchneedle
15 cm (6 in) lip-lock hoop
22 cm (9 in) square of fabric
fine steel crochet hook
fine sharp scissors
2 mm piece of plastic tubing (optional)
iron-on heat-transfer pen
You Can Wash It craft glue
Spinster braid maker (optional)

Threads

If using embroidery cotton, six strands are used throughout in the medium punchneedle. Acrylic yarns in single thickness in the medium needle work up beautifully with stunning results, as seen in the photograph.

Tracing pattern and colour guide for Christmas Decorations

actual size

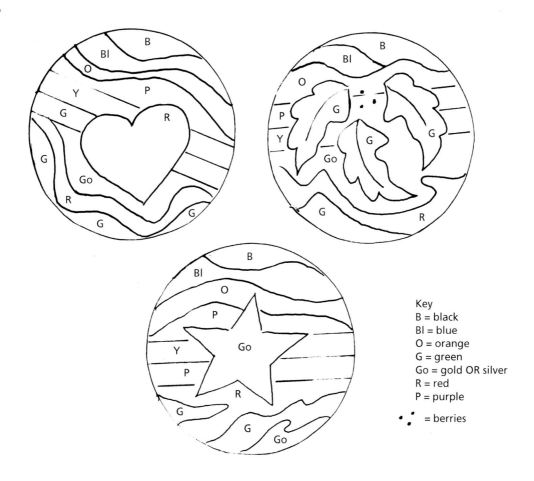

Key
B = black
Bl = blue
O = orange
G = green
Go = gold OR silver
R = red
P = purple
= berries

Embroidery cotton

Madeira	DMC
green 2704	green 3818
red 511	red 304
purple 2710	purple 550
blue 911	blue 798
yellow 113	yellow 743
orange 206	orange 946
black	black

Madeira Glamour, gold 2424, comes on a spool. It is usually used for decorative bobbin stitching or with an overlocker. Glamour is also available in the Pretty Punch range of acrylic threads.

Traditional punchneedle embroidery acrylic yarn

The conversions between yarns are not always exact but I have chosen colours that work well together.

Cameo	Pretty Punch
medium green 27	emerald green 66
orange 73	bright orange 73
dark lavender 37	popular purple 13
deep red 86	poinsettia red 62
blue 74	bright blue 51
gold yellow 45	bright lemon 55
black	black
silver metallic 619	silver MS

Preparation

Trace the three bauble designs onto the back of the fabric using your preferred method. The easiest way is with a heat-transfer pen.

Place the fabric in the hoop with the traced designs uppermost. Ensure that the fabric is extremely taut in the hoop and the hoop nut is done up very tight.

The circular outlines can become a little distorted when the fabric is stretched in the hoop. Pull on the fabric to adjust it so that the designs are as near to round as is possible.

TIPS

If the circles remain distorted, cut a circle the same size from clear acetate. Place this over the designs in the hoop and pull the outlines back into shape.

If you are working the decorations in acrylic yarn, and wish to finish them with braid, as in the photograph, replace the final 2 outline rows of silver metallic stitching with 2 rows of any other colour. The braid will not readily adhere to the silver metallic thread.

Embroidery

Follow the colour guide on the pattern.

Heart

The heart is worked in red with the needle tip set at No 2.

The rest of the design is worked at No 1.

Work 2 rows of metallic (or the acrylic colour of your choice) all the way around at No 1. Work the stitches for the outside row very close together to form a solid line of colour.

Holly leaves

Work the red berries with 10 stitches in a circle at No 2 (see Stitch Glossary).

Work the leaves at No 2. Work the veins first, in silver or gold, then work the green.

The remainder of the design is worked at No 1.

Work 2 rows of metallic (or the acrylic yarn of your choice) all the way around. Work the stitches close together.

Star

Work the star shape at No 2 with the gold thread or at No 1 with the silver thread.

The remainder is worked at No 1.

Work two rows of metallic (or the acrylic colour of your choice) all the way around. Work the stitches close together.

TIP

The Cameo silver metallic flows through the needle more readily than the acrylic yarn, leaving longer loops which can look too high in this design. An option for the silver areas is to work with a 2 mm piece of plastic tubing on the needle tip with the needle set at No 1. (If the loops do not then stay in place, shorten the plastic; see Pile Depth, page 13.)

Finishing

With the fabric still in the hoop, look at the front of the finished work to check if there are any long loops sticking up. Pull these *very carefully* through to the back with the fine steel crochet hook, taking care not to get the hook caught in other stitches.

Tidy the back and cut all the ends very, very short.

Remove the fabric from the hoop and pull the embroidery into shape.

Smear You Can Wash It craft glue over the entire back of the embroidery to about 6 mm (¼ in) outside the edge of teach design onto the fabric.

Allow to dry before carefully cutting each decoration away from the surrounding fabric. If by chance you accidentally cut some loops, simply trim the cut loop or add a little more glue

Diagram 1: Making loop at top of decoration

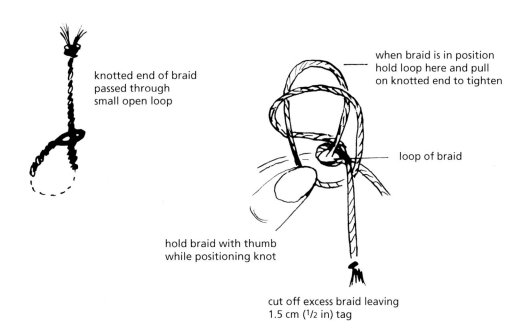

knotted end of braid
passed through
small open loop

when braid is in position
hold loop here and pull
on knotted end to tighten

loop of braid

hold braid with thumb
while positioning knot

cut off excess braid leaving
1.5 cm (¹/₂ in) tag

and push the cut loop back into place.

If using braid, glue it around each decoration.

Braid

See Braid Making in Stitch Glossary.

If the Spinster is used the gold braid is made with four 1 m (40 in) lengths of gold thread. Use six lengths if a thicker braid is preferred. When you remove the hook from the braid, hold the little loop formed by the hook open and pass the knotted end through to make a larger loop.

If using the finger method, four 50 cm (20 in) lengths of thread are required. Again, if you want a thicker braid more lengths of thread need to be added.

The multi-coloured braid made from the acrylic yarn is made using a 1 metre (40 in) length of each of the following colours—purple, green, blue, red, orange and yellow, with the addition of two lengths of silver metallic.

Leave the braid aside until you are ready to attach it to a decoration.

Work on a plastic sheet.

1   To attach a Spinster braid, with the wrong side of the decoration uppermost, mark the top with a pin. The loop with the braid passing through it is positioned at this spot. The loop is positioned facing towards the left of the decoration.

Put a little glue to halfway around on the right side of decoration. Push the braid onto the glued outside edge. Rest the decoration on the plastic sheet, with the braid pushed firmly against the glued edge. Take care to keep the plastic sheet free from glue which can get onto the front of the decoration.

Allow to dry before gluing the remaining half of the twisted thread into place.

When the braid is in place and dry, form a hanging loop approximately 5 cm (2 in) long at the top and tie a knot to hold it in place, following diagram 1. Work the knot into position to sit at the very top of the decoration.

Cut away the excess braid leaving a 1.5 cm (½ in) tag. Place glue on the end of the tag to prevent any fraying and press the tag firmly onto the back of the decoration. You can add a tassel or hanging beads to the bottom of the decorations as extra adornment.

2   To attach a finger braid is a little different. There is no loop at the end of the braid, only a knot. Glue the knot at the top of the decoration, leave to dry. Leave a 1.5 cm (½ in) gap free of glue immediately next to the knot. Continue with the previous instructions until the final knot-tying action. The braid is now glued entirely around the decoration up to the knot. Take the remaining length of braid and pass it from the front to the back through the small gap which was not glued. Finish the knot tying procedure as in the previous instructions.

Your beautiful Christmas decorations can be used as Christmas tree hangings, hung on a wide tartan ribbon or attached to a vine wreath, in a card, as a brooch or to decorate serviette rings, framed or used as fridge magnets. And of course as a gorgeous gift for very special people!

9 HANDSTAND CLOWN

This colourful clown is handstanding with joy, happy to be on a special little person's library bag. One clown is worked in six-stranded embroidery cotton and the other in tradition punchneedle embroidery acrylic yarn.

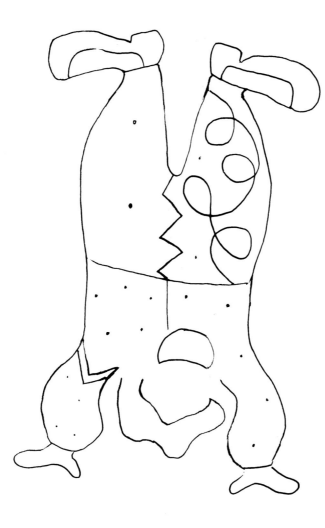

Tracing pattern for Handstand Clown

actual size

Materials

medium and small punchneedles

15 and 20 cm (6 and 8 in) lip-lock hoops

20 and 25 cm (8 and 10 in) squares of fabric

fine steel crochet hook

fine sharp scissors

iron-on transfer pen

You Can Wash It craft glue

sewing needle

Threads

Six strands of embroidery cotton are used throughout in the medium punchneedle (except for the face, where three strands are used in the small needle), or one thickness of acrylic yarn in the medium punchneedle.

Embroidery cotton

Madeira	DMC
green 1305	*green 701*
orange 206	*orange 946*
purple 2710	*purple 550*
red 511	*red 498*
blue 911	*blue 798*
yellow 113	*yellow 743*
black	*black*
white	*white*

Stitch guide

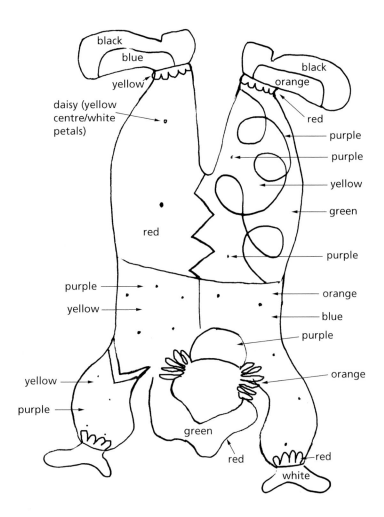

Traditional punchneedle embroidery acrylic yarn

The conversion from one acrylic yarn to the other is not always exact. Where a colour is not an absolute match I have chosen colours that work well together.

Cameo	Pretty Punch
medium green 27	peacock 74
orange 84	bright orange 73
dark lavender 37	popular purple 13
deep red 86	poinsettia red 61
radiant blue 10	bright blue 51
gold yellow 45	bright lemon 55
black	black
white	white

Preparation

Trace the clown design onto the back of the larger square of fabric. The face and ball are traced onto the back of the smaller square of fabric and worked separately, in the smaller hoop.

Handstand Clown worked with embroidery cotton.

Check the stretch of the fabric and place the designs upright with the most stretch of the fabric going up and down.

Place the larger fabric in the larger hoop with the traced clown design uppermost, ensuring that the fabric is extremely tight.

Embroidery

The entire clown is worked at No 1 with the exception of the frills, hat and hair.

Left trouser leg
The left leg is worked in red with two white daisies with yellow centres.

Work the daisies first. Work the centres on the marked dots with 15 stitches in a circle (figure 6, Stitch Glossary) in yellow at No1. To embroider the daisy petals (see diagram 1, and figure 11 in the Stitch Glossary) work 5 stitches from the centre. Work 3 stitches backwards. Leave the needle in the fabric and turn the work so that the centre is now closer to you. Cross over the first row you have worked and then work 3 stitches backwards. The reason for working this way is to have the straight side of the punchneedle always along the row just worked, which prevents loops on the front being accidentally punched through.

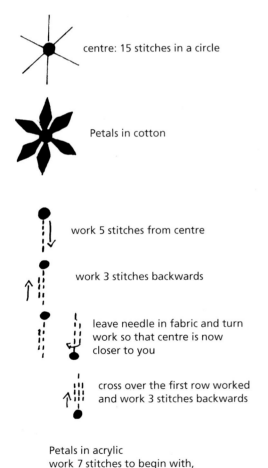

centre: 15 stitches in a circle

Petals in cotton

work 5 stitches from centre

work 3 stitches backwards

leave needle in fabric and turn work so that centre is now closer to you

cross over the first row worked and work 3 stitches backwards

Petals in acrylic
work 7 stitches to begin with,
then work 4 stitches on either side

Diagram 1: How to work the daisies

Note When using cotton, the first row of the daisy is made with 5 stitches and then 3 stitches on either side (see diagram 1). When using the acrylic yarn, there are 7 stitches to begin, with 4 stitches on either side.

Right trouser leg

The right leg is worked in green and yellow, with a purple swirl separating the colours, and two purple dots made with 10 stitches in a circle.

Jacket

The left side is worked in purple and yellow. Follow the stitch guide for the placement of the circles and lines. All circles are worked with 10 stitches. Two rows each of yellow and purple are embroidered for the V-shaped stripes. The right side is worked in blue and orange, with 20 stitches in a circle for the orange dots.

Neck frill

The dark line around the frill is worked in red. If using cotton, embroider 1 row with the needle set at No 3; if using acrylic yarn, embroider 2 rows at No 5. Fill the remaining area of the collar with green at No 1.

Sleeve and trouser frills

The frills on the sleeves are worked in 2 rows of red, with 6 stitches in each row, at No 5 for cotton and No 7 for acrylic yarn. At the bottom of the trousers the frill on one leg is worked in yellow, the other in red, using 2 rows of colour, with 8 stitches in each row at No 6 (cotton) and No 8 (acrylic yarn).

Shoes

The left shoe is worked in black and blue at No 1, the right shoe in black and orange.

Hat

Using purple, in cotton work at No 7 near the head and No 5 toward the edge; in acrylic yarn work at No 9 near the head and No 7 towards the edge.

Hands

Work in white at No 1.

Hair

In orange, work 2 rows of 5 stitches on either side of the head at No 12. Cut and trim the loops.

Face space

Fill in the area where the face will be placed with loops at No 1 in white. The completed face will be glued onto these loops, which raise the face to give it a three-dimensional appearance when completed.

Face

The face and ball are made on the smaller square of fabric. Trace the designs onto the fabric and place in the hoop with the traced designs uppermost.

Embroider the entire face in white at No 1, using three strands of embroidery cotton or one thickness of acrylic yarn in the small needle.

To make the red nose, take six strands of cotton or two thicknesses of acrylic yarn 20 cm (8 in) long. Tie a knot and work it into the centre of the thread. Thread the ends into a sewing needle and push the needle from the front to the back of the face on the dot marked for the nose. (Refer to diagram 6 in the Dandy Bear project.) Leave the knot at the front sitting up above the loops. Secure the ends of thread on the back with a smear of glue

The eyes and eyebrows are hand-embroidered with a needle and two strands of black cotton

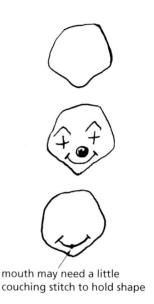

mouth may need a little couching stitch to hold shape

Clown face tracing pattern and stitch guide

tracing pattern

using straight stitches. The eyes are stitched like a plus sign, and the eyebrows in the shape of an upside-down V. See clown face stitch guide.

The mouth is stitched in red. Take a long stitch from one side of the nose to the other, leaving slack in the thread so that it sits in a curved line. The corners of the mouth are straight stitches at an angle. If the mouth lies straight, make a little couching stitch in the centre to hold it in a semi-circle to give the appearance of a happy chappy!

Ball

The ball is embroidered in the sculpted method using the medium needle. Refer back to Figure 15, sample 5 in the Stitch Glossary for instructions on sculpting. Set the needle tip at the lengths shown on the ball stitch guide.

Unlike all the other punchneedle embroidery, when sculpting, the traced pattern is put into the hoop facing down. You will be embroidering from inside the hoop. The loops made will be on the

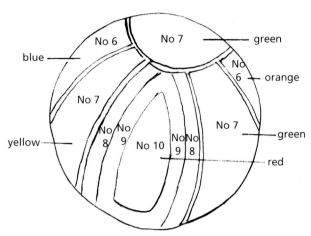

**Tracing pattern and stitch
guide for ball**

actual size

top of the hoop making them easier to trim.

When the embroidery is complete, remove the fabric from the hoop, cut, trim and shape the ball where necessary.

Glue over the back. Leave to dry. Cut out the ball and glue it into place, guided by the photograph.

Finishing

Spread a thin smear of You Can Wash It craft glue over the back of the face and leave to dry.

Cut the face away from the fabric close to the loops, taking care not to cut any loops. Position and glue the face into place over the white loops embroidered in the space for the face.

This delightful fellow can be framed.

If the clown is to be cut out, use the Appliqué method to attach it to a sweatshirt or, as in the photograph, to a child's library bag.

Three other clown designs in this series area available from Dancing Needle Designs (see Suppliers List). The four together look absolutely fabulous made into quilt blocks for a child's knee rug or a wall hanging.

10 DANCING BEAR

This dancing bear and his friend the dancing duck enjoy frolicking in a garden of flowers. The version in the photograph has been worked in Madeira embroidery cotton.

Tracing pattern for Dancing Bear
actual size

Materials

small and medium punchneedles

15 and 25 cm (6 and 10 in) lip-lock hoops

*fabric piece large enough to fit across the top of
    the blanket, plus a 22 cm (9 in) square of
    tightly woven fabric for appliqué version*

iron-on interfacing (optional)

wool blanketing

fabric doughnut

sharp embroidery scissors

very fine steel crochet hook

You Can Wash It craft glue

Water-erasable pen

iron-on transfer pen

sewing needle

Threads

Embroidery cotton

Madeira	DMC
brown 2103	brown 3045
pale brown 2102	pale brown 422
dark green 1504	dark green 937
pale green 1502	pale green 470
blue 911	blue 798
medium brown 2105	medium brown 869
yellow 113	yellow 743
red 210	red 666
grey 1802	grey 318
white	white

Traditional punchneedle embroidery acrylic yarn

The conversion from one acrylic yarn to the
other is not always exact. Where a colour is not
an absolute match I have chosen colours that
work well together.

Cameo	Pretty Punch
beige 54	light taupe 43
tan 55	medium taupe 30
dark aspen 26	dark aspen 68
aspen green 25	aspen green 67
blue 74	celestial blue 52
gold yellow 45	yellow gold 56
deep red 86	poinsettia red 62
light grey 63	silver grey 75
white	white

Preparation

The bear and his duck friend can be embroidered
directly onto the fabric chosen for the top of the
blanket. Decide whether this fabric will require
an iron-on interfacing to strengthen it, and
whether it needs to be protected with the
doughnut to prevent the hoop leaving a mark.

Alternatively, trace the bear and duck onto the
22 cm (9 in) square of fabric and work separately
as a cut out appliqué. If the appliqué method is
used, the remaining background embroidery is
worked on the fabric chosen for the top of the
blanket.

Trace the clouds, horizon line and spikes of
grass onto the front of the fabric.

Trace the remainder of the design onto the
back of fabric. Place the fabric in the hoop with
the back of the fabric uppermost.

Ensure that the fabric is extremely taut in the
hoop and the nut is done up very tight.

Embroidery

The areas embroidered in reverse punchneedle
embroidery are worked last of all. You may
choose to work these areas in traditional stem
stitch hand embroidery.

Bear

Three strands of embroidery cotton are used
throughout with the small punchneedle, or one
thickness of acrylic yarn with the medium
punchneedle, set at No 1 except where indicated.
The instructions refer to Madeira colours.
Substitute if using another yarn.

Key
duck: dark lines worked in grey
bear: dark internal lines and cross-hatched
areas worked in medium brown

• flowers

⌇ reverse punchneedle embroidery in pale green

⌇ reverse punchneedle embroidery in dark green

⌇ dark green

Body The main parts of the body are worked in brown 2103. The darker areas of shading are worked in medium brown 2105.

Mouth and nose With black work 10 stitches in a circle (see figure 6, Stitch Glossary) for the nose with the needle set at No 6.

The area indicated around the black nose and mouth is worked in brown 2103 with the needle set at No 7.

Remove the fabric from the hoop and shape the area around the black nose with sharp scissors to give a gentle rounded appearance. Leave the loops of the black nose uncut.

The mouth is stitched in with a sewing needle and black thread, using only 2 straight stitches. Do not pull the stitches tight but leave them loose to fall in a gentle curve.

Place fabric back into the hoop.

Eyes Work in black with 5 stitches in a circle for each eye. The white dot for the eye is made by taking a 20 cm (8 in) length of one strand of white cotton. Tie a knot in the thread and position the knot in the centre. Thread the two ends of thread through a sewing needle.

From the front, push the needle into the black part of the eye at about the position of 1 o'clock. Pull the needle through to the back and pull the thread until the knot at the front is at the same level as the black stitches. (See Dandy Bear, diagram 6.) Secure the thread at the back with a smear of glue.

Ears Use medium brown 2105 and work 20 stitches in a circle for the central area of the ears indicated by a dot on the pattern.

Scarf Work in blue 911 and then gently embroider dots randomly in yellow 113 (see figure 19, Stitch Glossary). Sometimes dots worked at the same length as the previously worked area will not show through. If this is your experience, work the dots with the needle set at No 2.

The fringe is worked at each end of the scarf with the needle set at No 6. Cut and trim the loops to form the fringe.

Duck

At No 1, work the body and head in white and grey where indicated on the stitch guide.

The beak and boots are worked in red. There is a small line of grey to separate the sole on one shoe only.

His little legs are worked in yellow.

Flowers

There are five flowers, four of which are worked with three strands of yellow 113 through the small needle. The fifth flower is bigger and worked with six strands in the medium needle.

Flower 1 This is merely a bud, worked with the needle set at No 1 with 10 stitches in a circle.

Flower 2 The centre is worked with 15 stitches in a circle with the needle set at No 1; then work 10 stitches all the way around at No 4.

Flowers 3 and 4 The centres are worked with 20 stitches in a circle with the needle set at No 1; then work 15 stitches all the way around at No 5 to make the petals.

Flower 5 Use six strands through the medium needle. The centre is worked with 20 stitches in a circle with the needle set at No 1; then work 12 stitches all the way around at No 7.

Greenery

The denser green areas under the tussocks and under the bear's and duck's feet are worked from the back, following the darker lines on the pattern, with three strands of dark green 1504 with the needle set at No 2.

Remove the fabric from the hoop and turn it over to complete the clumps of grass, stems, clouds and horizon line worked in reverse punchneedle embroidery. See the stitch guide.

The horizon line in pale green 1502 and the clouds in blue 911 are worked in reverse punchneedle embroidery. The stems linking the flowers are worked in reverse punchneedle embroidery with pale green 1502. The grass indicated by the wavy lines is worked with reverse punchneedle embroidery in pale green 1502. The grass indicated by the broken lines is worked in reverse punchneedle embroidery in dark green 1504.

Finishing

Remove the fabric from the hoop, pull it into shape and trim the ends of the threads on the back.

Because reverse punchneedle embroidery can get snagged and be easily pulled undone, as a precaution carefully lightly smear glue over the loops on the back of the reverse punchneedle embroidery and the flowers. Take care to ensure the glue is not put onto the fabric where there is a chance it can seep through to the front.

Attach the embroidered fabric to the top edge of the baby blanket and bind the edges with the same or a contrasting fabric.

If the bear and his friend have been embroidered on a separate square of fabric to be appliquéd, glue around the outside edges of the finished embroidery and leave to dry. Cut close to the edge. Spread glue completely over the back and position them in place among the flowers and greenery embroidered directly onto the blanket.

11 THE WICKER BASKET

One can reflect upon the charm of yesteryear on seeing a wicker basket full of pretty pink roses. The framed version is worked in Madeira embroidery cotton, that in the closeup photograph in traditional punchneedle embroidery acrylic yarn.

Tracing pattern for The Wicker Basket
actual size

Materials

15 cm (6 in) lip-lock hoop

20 cm (8 in) square of fabric

iron-on interfacing

sharp embroidery scissors

small and medium punchneedles

water-erasable pen

coloured iron-on transfer paper (optional)

small piece of clear acetate

2 mm of plastic tubing for needle tip

Threads

Embroidery cotton

Madeira	DMC
light green 1609	light green 581
medium green 1602	medium green 3363
green 1504	green 937
dark green 1601	dark green 3362
pale pink 808	pale pink 778
medium pink 809	medium pink 316
dark pink 810	dark pink 315

You can use any light tan thread equivalent to No 8 crochet cotton, such as Sullivan's crochet cotton, for the basket. A tightly twisted thread makes the basket look more authentic.

Traditional punchneedle embroidery acrylic yarn

The conversion from one acrylic yarn to the other is not always exact. Where a colour is not an absolute match I have chosen colours that work well together.

Cameo	Pretty Punch
medium avocado 825 (lustre)	aspen green 67
avocado 69	medium avocado 69
aspen green 25	aspen green 67
dark aspen 26	dark aspen 68
medium pink 130 (satin)	light mauve 5
medium pink 30	pink blush 20
dark pink 77	hot pink 2
tan 155 (satin)	tan No 8 crochet cotton
for basket	

Preparation

I used a plain cream polyviscose fabric onto which I ironed some delicate background colour using Rainbow colour transfer paper laid horizontally (see Painting Fabric, Chapter 2). This

Key
stems medium green 1602
flowers:dark pink 810
medium pink 809
light pink 808

●   placement for flowers

    bud

    satin stitch

    fern stitch light green 1609

    reverse punchneedle embroidery

    longer stitches in reverse
    punchneedle embroidery

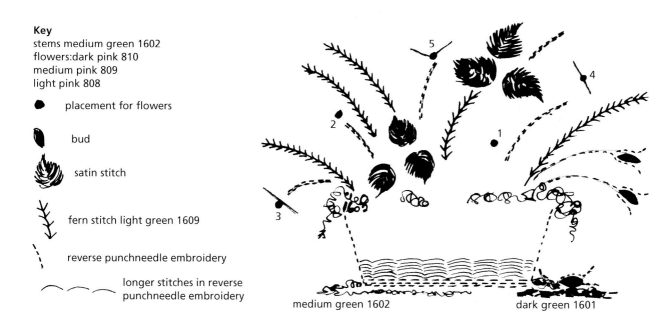

medium green 1602   dark green 1601

Stitch guide

technique is ideal for those who are hesitant about painting their own background colours. I traced the basket onto the green strip of colour which was transferred to the fabric.

Before starting, re-read the section on marking the straight grain of the fabric (Chapter 2). Trace the outline of the basket onto the *front* of the fabric, preferably with a water-erasable pen or a very fine lead pencil. It is important to have the basket marked very straight on the fabric so that the completed embroidery looks straight when placed into a frame. An easy way of drawing the outline is to cut a template of the basket from stiff paper or acetate; this can be easily aligned with the grain of the fabric and traced around. Trace the vertical lines onto the front of the fabric.

Trace the remainder of the design (leaves, buds and stems) onto the back of the fabric.

Place the fabric in the hoop with the tracing of the basket uppermost. Take care when tightening the nut on the hoop not to mark the fabric. The use of a doughnut gives added protection (see Hoop Techniques).

Basket

This is worked from the front of the fabric in reverse punchneedle embroidery (figure 7, a, Stitch Glossary).

Use the medium needle set at No 1 with the crochet cotton (or the satin acrylic yarn).

Commence at the top left corner and work all around the outline of the basket. Work 2 rows close together inside the bottom edge of the basket.

Change the needle tip to No 3 to embroider the longer stitches making up the horizontal weave of the basket. Some length of the thread is taken up for the stitch but there still needs to be sufficient thread to form a long enough loop to stay in the fabric. Check the back of the fabric to see that the loops are long enough to stay in place. If not, lengthen the needle tip.

Starting at the bottom and working toward the top of the basket, work horizontal lines backwards and forwards to form the weave of the basket. Use the vertical lines in the basket as guides for the length of your stitches. At the end of each row, take a very small stitch along the

Diagram 1: Working the buds (enlarged)

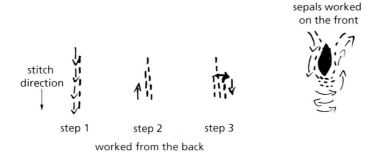

basket outline and then work the next row. Keep these rows close together. When working like this the long stitches take on a natural, gentle curve which gives added dimension to the weave of the basket. Keep the beginning and end of each row inside the outline of stitches.

Pull all of the beginning and ending threads through to the back. Trim the ends of the threads.

Remove the fabric from the hoop, turn it over and replace it tightly in the hoop. The back of the fabric is now uppermost in preparation for embroidering the flowers.

Flowers

These instructions refer to working with Madeira cottons. Substitute if using other threads.

The flowers are worked with three strands of cotton using the small punchneedle. Before beginning, refer to figure 6, Stitch Glossary.

Flowers 1 and 2 First row, at No 1 with dark pink 810, work 15 stitches in a circle.

Second row, at No 3 with medium pink 809, work all the way around.

Third row, at No 4 work all the way around with medium pink 809.

Fourth row, at No 5 with pale pink 808, work all the way around.

Fifth row, at No 6 work all the way around with pale pink 808.

Flowers 3 and 4 These are both worked in the same way as flowers 1 and 2, except that rows 2, 3, 4 and 5 are only worked three-quarters of the way around the centre circle. Note the way these flowers are facing in the photographs. Work only to the lines marked on the pattern.

Flower 5 This is worked the same as flower 1, but this time work a little more than three-quarters of the way around the centre circle, using the lines marked on the pattern as a guide.

Buds See diagram 1, and figure 11 in Stitch Glossary.

To give a finer appearance to the three buds, place a 2 mm piece of plastic tubing on the small needle to make the loops shorter and work at No 1. See Pile Depth.

For each bud, in medium pink 809, work 5 stitches forward (step 1). Work 3 stitches backwards on the left side and close to the row just worked (step 2). Leave the needle in the fabric and turn the hoop. Take a stitch across the first row worked and work 3 stitches close to and along the left side of the first row (step 3). The green sepals are worked later.

Note the fallen bud near the base of the basket. Work this bud in the same way.

Remove the fabric from the hoop, turn it over and replace it tightly in the hoop with the right

The Wicker Basket worked in embroidery cotton.

side of the fabric uppermost in preparation for working the leaves and ferns which are worked in reverse punchneedle embroidery.

Leaves

The leaves are worked mostly with three strands of cotton using the small punchneedle, except for the fern which is worked with two strands. The leaves are embroidered in satin stitch (figure 8, Stitch Glossary), which is worked from the front with long straight stitches angled to give effect. Start with the needle set at No 2. If the stitches do not hold in place, alter the length. Keep a check on the back to see if the loops are sufficiently long enough to hold in place.

See stitch guide for placement of colours.

The leaves worked in green 1504 have darker veins worked over them in green 1601. Work the veins similarly to the ferns (figure 7, b, Stitch Glossary), but work backwards, starting at the base of the leaf with the stitches placed further apart. This highlighting adds more interest to the design.

Green sepals around the buds

Work reverse punchneedle embroidery with medium green 1602 at No 1. Referring to diagram 1, start at the left sepal, stitch to the base of the bud and then work backwards and forwards across the base to form the calyx. Leave the needle in the hoop, turn the work and stitch along the other side of the bud to form the other sepal.

Ferns

The ferns are embroidered using the open textured satin stitch (figure 18, Stitch Glossary).

Set the needle at No 2. Embroider the ferns with two strands of light green 1609, starting at the bottom and working backwards. Take a stitch to the left and return to the centre. Take a stitch to the right and return to the centre, continuing until the area to be worked is finished. Check the back of the piece to see that there is a long enough loop left on the back to hold in the fabric. If the loop seems too short, lengthen the needle tip.

Green at base of basket

Follow the lines on the pattern and use two tones of green: medium green 1602 is worked on the side of the basket under flower 3; the darker green 1601 is used to form a shadow on the side under the buds.

Stems

Use medium green 1602 and No 1. Under flower 5 work a few small straight stitches across in a semi-circle to form the calyx before stitching the stem. The stems are worked in 2 rows—the first forward and the second backward, in reverse punchneedle embroidery. The backward stitching sits on top of the first row to give thickness to the stem.

The stems for the buds have only 1 row of stitching.

Loops along top of basket

This final part of the embroidery is worked from the back. With green 1602 punch in a few loops along the top of the basket at No 3 and some

loops to overflow the sides of the basket, varying the needle from No 6 to No 1. Have a look at the photographs to see the placement and amount of stitching required.

Tips for working with acrylic yarn

The needle lengths are the same as for the cotton instructions, the design is worked the same way, and the colourways are directly transposed from cotton to acrylic.

Note the following exceptions:
- Use the acrylic yarn through the medium needle.
- Use medium avocado 825 (lustre) for the ferns through the small needle.
- Use one strand of tan 155 (satin) in the small needle for the basket.
- Use two strands of medium pink 130 (satin) in the medium needle for the final 2 rows of each of the flowers.

Finishing

Remove the fabric from the hoop and pull the embroidery into shape. Trim the ends of the threads on the back.

When the embroidery is completed there will be spaces where the light background fabric shows through the design. These pale areas can be coloured in delicately with a fabric pen or paint. I most often use Derwent watercolour pencils or Jo Sonja fabric paints. Alternatively, embroider some extra loops into these areas, varying the length between No 1 and No 2.

Trim the ends of the threads on the back to prevent them showing through the fabric when the piece is framed.

Press around the embroidered area taking care that the iron does not slide over the embroidery.

Place fine wadding or pellon under the fabric before framing to provide a soft bed for the loops from the reverse punchneedle embroidery to nestle into. Frame and enjoy.

12 SCARF TOGGLES

These stunning scarf toggles are a superb idea to hold your scarf in just the right place. Your friends will be envious so you need to prepare to be making many for gifts.
Although these two designs look vastly different they are worked from an almost identical base. The turquoise, blue and pink Beauty is worked with Rajmahal art silks and silk ribbon, the gorgeous Autumn Tones is worked with Cameo acrylic yarn. You can, if you prefer, turn these pieces into brooches by adding a backing and a brooch pin.

Materials

15 cm (6 in) lip-lock hoop

20 cm (8 in) square of dark fabric

sharp embroidery scissors

medium and large punchneedles

sewing needle for beads

You Can Wash It craft glue

white or coloured dressmaker's carbon

4 mm silk ribbon to match Rajmahal threads

small beads to match

10 x 7.5 cm (4 x 3 in) dark fabric to make toggle

Threads

Rajmahal art silks

vibrant musk 184

cossack blue 122

peacock green 165

imperial purple 115

charcoal 29

For the two areas of 4 mm silk ribbon, any matching colour can be used. I used Colourstream hand-dyed silk ribbon, with one area in mauve/pink/purple shades, the other in green/emerald/blue shades.

Traditional punchneedle embroidery acrylic yarn

The colour conversion from one acrylic yarn to another is not always exact. Where colours are not an absolute match I have chosen colours that work well together.

Cameo	Pretty Punch
dark brown 62	*dark brown 70*
taupe 59	*rusty brown 29*
brandy 39	*burnt orange 39*
avocado 69	*medium avocado 69*
raspberry wine 72	*terracotta 38*

Preparation

When completed the scarf toggles will be cut away from the background fabric. As the outside rows are black or dark colours it is better to work the embroidery on black fabric. If a pale fabric is chosen, the edges will show when cut and detract from the beauty of the completed embroidery (see Appliqué, Chapter 4).

Trace the design onto the back of fabric using dressmaker's carbon.

Place the fabric in the hoop with the tracing uppermost. Ensure that the fabric is extremely tight in the hoop.

Use the stitch guides for the placement of colours.

Beauty

Working with Rajmahal art silks, use the full thickness of the thread through the medium punchneedle. Set the needle at No 1.

Outline the sections in charcoal.

Fill in the various thread colours following the stitch guide.

The two areas of silk ribbon loops are worked with the large punchneedle set at No 10. (I suggest you refresh your memory by reading Working with Silk Ribbons at the end of Chapter 2.)

Tracing pattern for Beauty

actual size

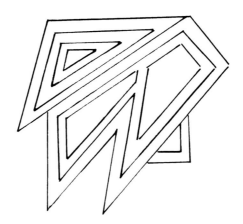

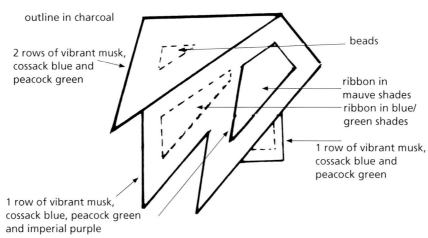

outline in charcoal

2 rows of vibrant musk,
cossack blue and
peacock green

beads

ribbon in
mauve shades

ribbon in blue/
green shades

1 row of vibrant musk,
cossack blue and
peacock green

1 row of vibrant musk,
cossack blue, peacock green
and imperial purple

Stitch guide for Beauty in Rajmahal art silks

Using a sewing needle and matching thread, stitch through each ribbon loop, then thread a bead onto the needle. Pull the loops down slightly by pulling the thread to the back so that the ribbon loops become shorter and scrunched up.

Stitch beads atop each other so that there is a dense cluster in the area marked on the pattern.

Finishing

Trim the ends on the back.

Glue all over the back with You Can Wash It craft glue. Allow to dry.

Cut the design away from the fabric.

Take one thickness of each Rajmahal colour and a thread of gold (optional) to make a braid. (See Braid making at the end of the Stitch Glossary.) Stitch or glue the braid in place around the edge, and attach the embroidery to the toggle back, either by gluing it into place or by hand stitching.

You can make a backing and add a brooch pin as an alternative for using this design.

Tracing pattern for Autumn Tones

actual size

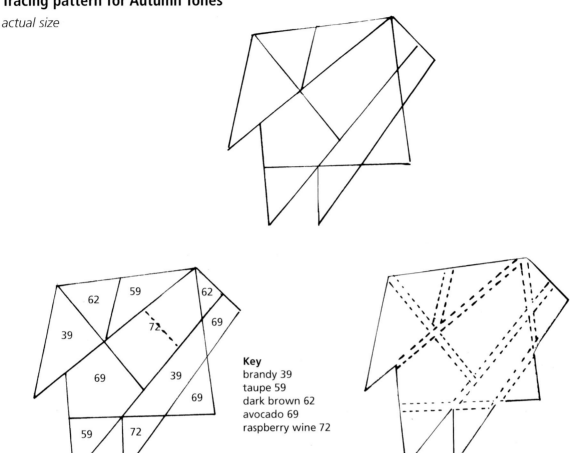

Key
brandy 39
taupe 59
dark brown 62
avocado 69
raspberry wine 72

spaces between broken lines left unworked

Stitch guide for Autumn Tones in acrylic yarn

Autumn Tones

This piece is sculpted. (See sculpting techniques in the Stitch Glossary.)

Set the needle at No 7 to embroider the whole piece. Follow the placement of the colours on the stitch guide. Once the embroidery is completed, sculpt the piece using the photograph for guidance. In the largest area, worked in raspberry wine 72, cut the loops much shorter in the position indicated by the dotted line to give added interest to the finished piece.

Outline each area after it has been cut and sculpted, using the same colour with the needle set at No 1. Work the stitches very close together.

Finishing

Trim the ends on the back.

Glue all over the back with You Can Wash It craft glue. Allow to dry.

Cut the design away from the fabric and attach it to the toggle back.

Making the toggle

Follow the directions in diagrams 1 to 8 to make the toggle.

127

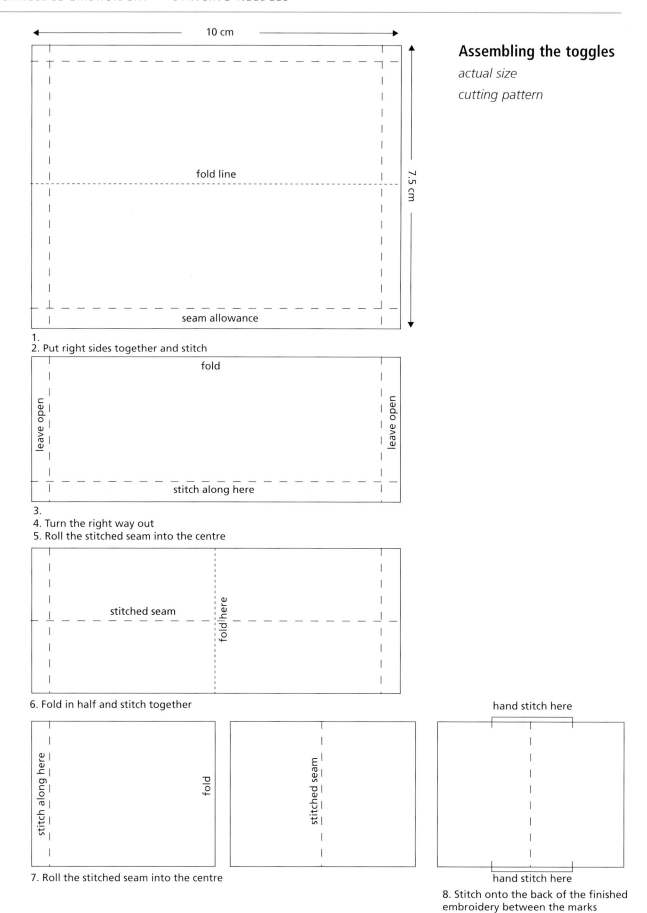

10 cm

7.5 cm

fold line

seam allowance

Assembling the toggles
actual size
cutting pattern

1.
2. Put right sides together and stitch

fold

leave open

leave open

stitch along here

3.
4. Turn the right way out
5. Roll the stitched seam into the centre

stitched seam

fold here

6. Fold in half and stitch together

stitch along here

fold

stitched seam

7. Roll the stitched seam into the centre

hand stitch here

hand stitch here

8. Stitch onto the back of the finished embroidery between the marks

13 THE FLOWER GARDEN

This gorgeous garden of flowers blooms all year round. A joy to embroider, this will become a treasured keepsake. The embroidery on the gold box was worked in Rajmahal art silk, on the black box in Cameo acrylic yarn.

Materials

20 cm (8 in) lip-lock hoop

25 cm (10 in) square fabric

sharp embroidery scissors

small and medium punchneedles (Rajmahal
    art silk)

medium and large punchneedles (acrylic yarn)

water-erasable pen

Fray Stop (optional)

2 mm piece of plastic tubing (optional)

satin-covered oval box, 14 x 10 cm (5 ½ x 4 in)

Threads

There is no direct colour transfer between the Rajmahal art silk colours and the Cameo acrylic colours used in this project.

There is little similarity between the shimmering colours of the Rajmahal embroidery and the brighter, flatter-looking colours of the acrylic piece, but both are gorgeous in their own right when the embroidery is completed.

Preparation

Trace the design onto the back of fabric.

Place the fabric in the hoop with the tracing uppermost. Ensure that the fabric is extremely tight in the hoop.

Embroidery with Rajmahal art silks

The medium punchneedle with six strands of thread is used throughout, except for the leaves and the background, which are worked with three strands in the small punchneedle.

TIPS

The Rajmahal thread is shiny and slippery. The medium needle can leave an opening between the fibres of the fabric through which the ends of the shiny thread can slip to the front. Where the slipping of thread is a problem apply a small amount of Fray Stop or You Can Wash It craft glue to the end of the thread on the back of the work, taking care that none seeps through to the front of the fabric.

A small knot tied at the end of the thread after threading the needle will hold the beginning threads in place and prevents them working their way to the front of the fabric. Remember, though, where you are working reverse punchneedle embroidery you will need to push the needle through the fabric, take the end tag of thread to the back of the fabric and then tie the knot.

Rajmahal art silk	Cameo acrylic	Pretty Punch acrylic
grape 243	cranberry 19	terracotta 38
dusky rose 241	flaming orange 38	watermelon 742
damask rose 742	cantaloupe 42	peach 42
white 96	white	white
moroccan gold 94	gold yellow 45	bright lemon 55
winter white 90	baby yellow 43	baby maize 19
maidenhair 521	aspen green 25	aspen green 67
green earth 421	dark aspen 26	dark aspen 68
bluebell 121	blue 74	bright blue 51
dainty lilac 111	light lavender 36	dark lavender 8
purple dusk 113	dark lavender 37	popular purple 13
	orchid 4	orchid 9

**Tracing pattern for
The Flower Garden**

actual size

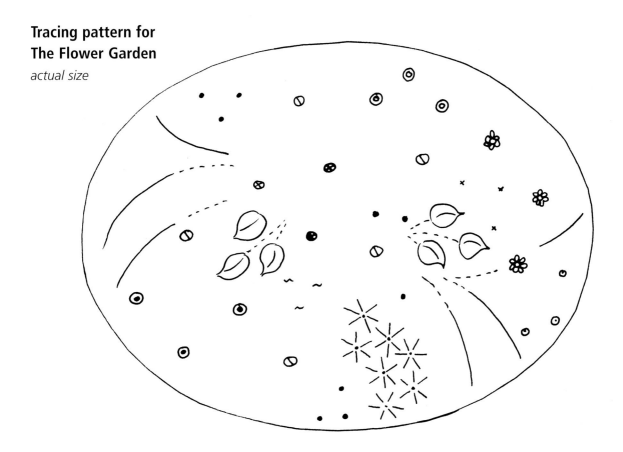

Flowers

These are all worked with the medium punchneedle and six strands of thread.

Flower 1 For these five daisies, set the punchneedle at No 1 and work 10 stitches in a circle in moroccan gold 94 (figure 6, Stitch Glossary).

Change thread to white 96 and the punchneedle length to No 10; mark the start for the next round of stitches with the water-erasable pen. Work all the way around the circle. Work a second row at No 10.

In the Rajmahal silk, the petals on the daisy flowers curl up; to get them to stay open, work 2 rows of reverse punchneedle embroidery (see figure 7, a, Stitch Glossary) from the front of the design, around the yellow centre, after the 2 rows of white petals have been worked.

Turn the hoop over. Thread with moroccan gold 94. Set the punchneedle at No 1 and begin the row by pulling the starting thread through to the back. Work the first row around the centre loops, punching the needle in at the base of each of the loops. The second row is worked close to the first with the stitches worked over the white loops. It is this row of stitching which holds the petals open. Pull the ending thread through to the back and cut.

Cut each white loop separately to give the daisy appearance.

Flower 2 These three flowers are worked in grape 243 with a dusky rose 241 centre (2a); dusky rose 241 with a grape 243 centre (2b), and damask rose 742 with a winter white 90 centre (2c).

To work the centres, set the punchneedle at No 2 and work 20 stitches in a circle using the centre colour.

Stitch guide

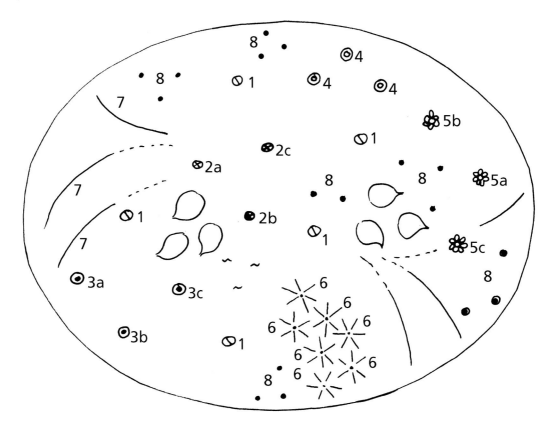

Change thread colour and the punchneedle length to No 10; mark the start for the next round of stitches with the water-erasable pen. Work all the way around the circle. Work a second row at No 7 all the way around.

Flower 3 These three flowers are worked in grape 243 with a dusky rose 241 centre (3a); dusky rose 241 with a grape 243 centre (3b), and damask rose 742 with a winter white 90 centre (3c)

To work the centres, set the punchneedle at No 2 and work 10 stitches in a circle using the centre colour.

Change thread colour and the punchneedle length to No 7; mark the start for the next round of stitches with the water erasable pen. Work all the way around the circle. Work a second row at No 7 all the way around.

One row of reverse punchneedle embroidery is worked around the centre loops to help keep the outer loops of petals open.

Turn the hoop over. Thread with the colour used for the centre. Set the punchneedle at No 1 and begin pulling the starting thread through to the back. Work around the centre loops, punching the needle in at the base of the loops. Pull the ending thread through to the back and cut.

Flower 4 These three flowers are worked in a single colour—one each in grape 243, dusky rose 241 and damask rose 742.

Set the punchneedle at No 3 and work 10 stitches in a circle.

Change to No 2; mark the start for the next round of stitches with the water-erasable pen. Work all the way around the circle. Change to

No 1 and work all the way around the circle.

Altering the setting of the punchneedle gives a domed effect to the completed flower.

Flower 5 These three flowers are worked in grape 243 with a dusky rose 241 centre (5a); dusky rose 241 with a grape 243 centre (5b), and damask rose 742 with a winter white 90 centre (5c).

Set the punchneedle at No 1 and work 20 stitches in a circle using the centre colour.

Change thread colour and the punchneedle length to No 3; mark the start for the next round of stitches with the water-erasable pen. Work all the way around the circle. Work a second row at No 9.

Flower 6 The seven star-shaped flowers on the front of the piece (figure 12, Stitch Glossary) are worked in dusky rose 241, damask rose 742, grape 243 and winter white 90. Refer to the photograph for their positions. These flowers are worked from the front.

Set the punchneedle at No 2. Begin in the centre of the flower by pulling the starting thread through to the back. Work each petal with a length of approximately 6 mm (¼ in) from the centre and out, and then back to the centre. Repeat. Each petal will have a double layer of stitching. If the loops on the back pull out,

increase the punchneedle length to No 3.

Flower 7 For each of the six spikes of lavender, thread the punchneedle with dainty lilac 111 and set at No 2. work from the back.

Punch the needle into the fabric near the tip of the spike (see diagram 1a). Work 2 stitches along centre line. Work 2 small stitches up and out to the left. Return to the centre by working 2 stitches over the previously formed stitches.

Work 2 small stitches up and out to the right. Return to the centre by working 2 stitches over the previously formed stitches.

Work 1 small stitch on the centre line.

Repeat the last three actions until the lavender spike is the desired length.

Work the base of the spike with only 1 stitch to either side.

The tip is worked in purple dusk 113 (see diagram 1b). Punch the needle into the same hole as the beginning stitch. Take a small backward stitch along the centre line. Then make a stitch forward but out to the left of the centre line. Take the next stitch in line with the last stitch and place it to the right of the centre line. This area is worked in a triangle to form the tip of the spike. Turn the work over to check that the stitches are close enough together to form a solid area of colour like a tiny arrowhead. Add more stitches if necessary.

Diagram 1: Lavender

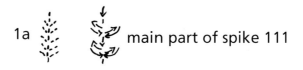

1a   main part of spike 111

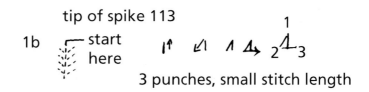

tip of spike 113

1b   start here

3 punches, small stitch length

Flower 8 These six groups of small flowers are made with the punchneedle set at No 1, working 10 stitches in a circle, in bluebell 121, winter white 90, damask rose 742 and grape 243. Be guided by the photograph for the placement of colour.

Leaves

These six leaves are worked in satin stitch (figure 8, Stitch Glossary), with three strands of green earth 521 in the small punchneedle.

The leaves are worked from the front of the fabric with long straight stitches angled to give effect. Start with the needle set at No 2 but if the loops do not hold in place alter the length.

Work from the base of the leaf to the tip, shortening the stitches toward the tip and changing to a shorter needle length to prevent a lot of bulk forming at the back. Change the needle to No 2 to complete the other side of the leaf. Pull the starting and finishing threads to the back of the work and trim.

Background

This is worked in meandering stitch (figure 9, Stitch glossary), using three strands of maidenhair 521 in the small punchneedle at No 1. If you feel that the loops for the background grass look too long, place the 2 mm piece of plastic tubing on the needle to shorten the loops (see Pile Depth, page 13) to make the background look more 'lawn-like'.

Stems

These are indicated by the dotted lines. Use three strands of green earth 421 in the small punchneedle and work the stems in reverse punchneedle embroidery at No 1 from the front.

Embroidery with acrylic yarn

Use the medium punchneedle with the acrylic yarn, but note that the lavender spike is worked with the large punchneedle.

Flowers

These are all worked with the medium punchneedle and acrylic yarn.

Flower 1 For these five daisies, set the punchneedle at No 3 and work 10 stitches in a circle in gold yellow 45 (figure 6, Stitch Glossary).

Change thread to white and the punchneedle length to No 12; mark the start for the next round of stitches with the water-erasable pen. Work all the way around the circle. Work a second row at No 12.

To get the daisy petals to open out wide and full, work 2 rows of reverse punchneedle embroidery (see figure 7, a, Stitch Glossary) from the front of the design, around the yellow centre after the 2 rows of white petals have been worked.

To do this, turn the hoop over. Thread with gold yellow 45. Set the punchneedle at No 3 and begin the row by pulling the starting thread through to the back. Work the first row around the centre loops, punching the needle in at the base of the loops. The second row is worked close to the first with the stitches worked over the white loops. It is this row of stitching which holds the petals open. Pull the ending thread through to the back and cut.

Cut each white loop separately to give the daisy appearance.

Flower 2 These three flowers are worked in cranberry 19 with a flaming orange 38 centre (2a); flaming orange 38 with a cranberry 19 centre (2b), and cantaloupe 42 with a baby yellow 43 centre (2c).

Set the punchneedle at No 4 and work 20 stitches in a circle using the centre colour.

Change thread colour and the punchneedle length to No 12; mark the start for the next round of stitches with the water-erasable pen. Work all the way around the circle. Work a second row at No 9.

Flower 3 These three flowers are worked in cranberry 19 with a flaming orange 38 centre (3a); flaming orange 38 with a cranberry 19 centre (3b), and cantaloupe 42 with a baby yellow 43 centre (3c)

Set the punchneedle at No 4 and work 10 stitches in a circle using the centre colour.

Change thread colour and the punchneedle length to No 9; mark the start for the next round of stitches with the water-erasable pen. Work all the way around the circle. Work a second row at No 9.

One row of reverse punchneedle embroidery is worked around the centre loops to give added interest to the flower centres.

Turn the hoop over. Thread with the colour used for the centre. Set the punchneedle at No 3 and begin pulling the starting thread through to the back. Work around the centre loops, punching the needle in at the base of the loops. Pull the ending thread through to the back and cut.

Flower 4 These three flowers are worked in a single colour—one each in cranberry 19, flaming orange 38 and cantaloupe 42.

Set the punchneedle at No 5 and work 10 stitches in a circle.

Change to No 4; mark the start for the next round of stitches with the water-erasable pen. Work all the way around the circle. Change to No 3 and work all the way around the circle.

Flower 5 These three flowers are worked in cranberry 19 with a flaming orange 38 centre (5a); flaming orange 38 with a cranberry 19 centre (5b), and cantaloupe 42 with a baby yellow 43 centre (5c).

Set the punchneedle at No 3 and work 20 stitches in a circle using the centre colour.

Change thread colour and the punchneedle length to No 5; mark the start for the next round of stitches with the water-erasable pen. Work all the way around the circle. Work a second row at No 11.

Flower 6 The seven star-shaped flowers on the front of the piece (figure 12, Stitch Glossary) are worked in flaming orange, cantaloupe, cranberry and baby yellow. Refer to the photograph for their positions.

Set the punchneedle at No 4. Begin in the centre of the flower by pulling the starting thread through to the back. Work each petal with a length of approximately 6 mm (¼ in) from the centre and out, and then back to the centre. Repeat. Each petal will have a double layer of

stitching. If the stitches pull out, increase the punchneedle length to No 5.

Flower 7 the lavender is worked with two colours, orchid 4 and light lavender 36 threaded at the same time through the large needle set at No 3. This is to get a truer colour for the flower (neither colour alone is a good match for lavender, but together they are fine).

Punch the needle into the fabric near the tip of the spike (see diagram 1a). Work 2 stitches along centre line. Work 2 small stitches up and out to the left. Return to the centre by working 2 stitches over the previously formed stitches.

Work 2 small stitches up and out to the right. Return to the centre by working 2 stitches over the previously formed stitches.

Work 1 small stitch on the centre line.

Repeat the last three actions until the lavender spike is the desired length.

Work the base of the spike with only 1 stitch to either side.

The tip is worked with two strands of dark lavender 37 in the large punchneedle (see diagram 1b). Punch the needle into the same hole as the beginning stitch. Take a small backward stitch along the centre line. Then make a stitch forward but out to the left of the centre line. Take the next stitch in line with the last stitch and place it to the right of the centre line. This area is worked in a triangle to form the tip of the spike. Turn the work over to check that the dark lavender stitches are close enough together to form a solid area of colour like a tiny arrowhead. Add more stitches if necessary.

Flower 8 These six groups of small flowers are made with the punchneedle set at No 3, working 10 stitches in a circle, in blue 74, baby yellow 43, cantaloupe 42 and cranberry 19. Be guided by the photograph in your placement of colour.

Leaves

These six leaves are worked in satin stitch (figure 8, Stitch Glossary), in dark aspen green 26.

The leaves are worked from the front of the fabric with long straight stitches angled to give effect. Start with the needle set at No 3 but if the stitches do not hold in place alter the length.

Work from the base of the leaf to the tip, shortening the stitches toward the tip and changing to a shorter needle length to prevent a lot of bulk forming at the back. Pull the starting and finishing threads to the back of the work and trim.

Background

This is worked in meandering stitch (figure 9, Stitch glossary), using three strands of thread in the small punchneedle at No 1. The green background uses two colours with the punchneeedle set at No 2 with aspen green 25 initially; then work dark aspen 26 in meandering stitch over this. The reason I suggest this is that the greens in the acrylic colour range are not suitable individually for a design such as this. With the darker green worked over the lighter one, the background becomes more realistic.

Stems

These are indicated by the dotted lines. Use dark aspen 26 and work the stems in reverse punchneedle embroidery at No 2.

Finishing

These delightful embroideries have been used atop satin-covered oval boxes, purchased already covered. The lid for the box comes already padded, but I find it better to provide additional padding with two layers of pellon cut to shape.

Remove the fabric from the hoop and stretch it in all directions to straighten the embroidery.

Trace the shape of the box top and outline on the fabric the area to be covered.

Cut the embroidery away from the fabric, leaving about 30 mm (1 ¼ in) allowance to turn under.

If you need to make your own padded top, cut a piece of strong cardboard and two pieces of pellon the same shape as the lid of the box.

Centre the embroidery over the covered top (or over the pellon and cardboard) and either lace the turn-under allowance tightly or glue it into place on the back of the cardboard. The same method can be used as described in Overflowing Cornucopia.

Glue the padded embroidery to the top of the box.

You may wish to trim the box with braid, taking a full thickness of each of the colours used in the acrylic yarns or the Rajmahal silks to make each braid. (See Braid Making in Stitch Glossary.)

What a lovely piece of embroidery to keep and treasure or to give to a special friend.

14 RIBBON HEART

A delightful flower-filled heart beautifully decorates an album cover. This design is worked in Madeira Decora rayon thread and YLI and Kakoonda silk ribbons.

Tracing pattern and stitch guide for Ribbon Heart
actual size

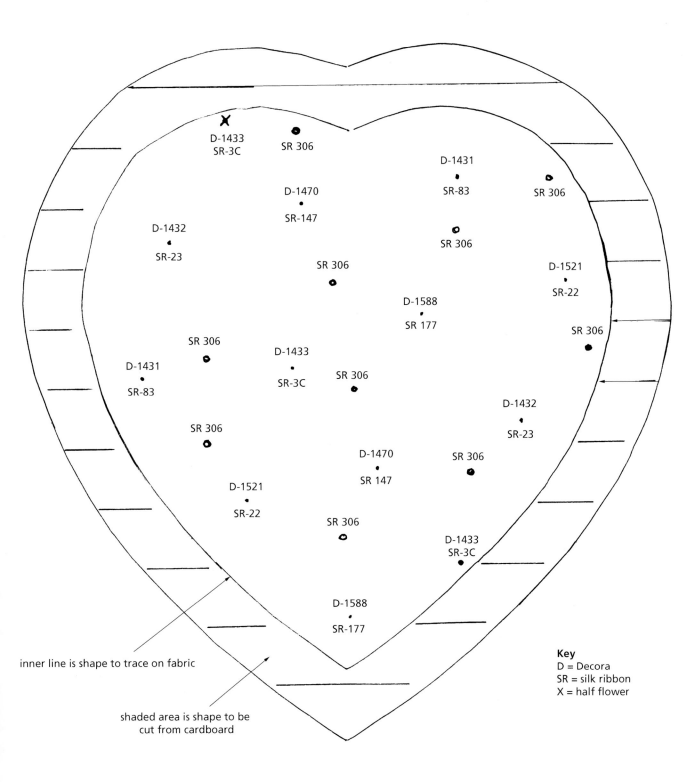

D-1433
SR-3C

SR 306

D-1431
SR-83

SR 306

D-1470
SR-147

D-1432
SR-23

SR 306

D-1521
SR-22

SR 306

D-1588
SR 177

SR 306

D-1433
SR-3C

SR 306

D-1431
SR-83

SR 306

D-1432
SR-23

D-1521
SR-22

D-1470
SR 147

SR 306

SR 306

D-1433
SR-3C

D-1588
SR-177

inner line is shape to trace on fabric

shaded area is shape to be
cut from cardboard

Key
D = Decora
SR = silk ribbon
X = half flower

139

Materials

medium and large punchneedles

20 cm (8 in) lip-lock hoop

30 cm (12 in) square of tightly woven fabric

You Can Wash It craft glue

fine lead pencil

water-erasable pen

sharp embroidery scissors

small plastic ruler

cardboard (for heart-shaped frame)

pellon (enough to pad frame, cover and to place under silk ribbon flowers)

fabric for cover and to cover heart-shaped frame

photograph album

Threads

The flower centres are worked with four strands of Madeira Decora, a lovely shiny rayon thread which looks wonderful with the silk ribbon. You can of course use any similar thread for the centres, or substitute six strands of embroidery cotton. The colours listed below for the cottons are approximate colour conversions to the Decora rayon.

I have used YLI silk ribbon and some ribbons from the Kakoonda hand-dyed range. You can use any 4 mm silk ribbon that will flow easily through the large punchneedle (see Silk Ribbons, page 65). Alternatively, use a 2 mm silk ribbon through a smaller punchneedle and work the flowers a little closer together. In this case, extra flowers may need to be worked to fill the area. (I suggest you refresh your memory by reading Tips for Working with Silk Ribbon on page 26.)

Silk ribbons

4 mm YLI in colours 83, 22, 23, 147, 177

Kakoonda 3C, a variegated hand-dyed mauve-toned ribbon; or substitute with YLI 178

Kakoonda green 306; or substitute with YLI 20

Allow 1.5 metres (60 in) of ribbon for each flower

Preparation

Embroider the flowers on the 30 cm (12 in) square of fabric which will need to be cut 15 mm (½ in) larger than the heart shape at the completion of the embroidery. The edges will be covered over with the frame.

Trace the heart shape onto the back of the fabric. Mark the dots showing the position of each flower. With the tracing uppermost, place the fabric tightly in the hoop.

Embroidery

Iron the ribbons if necessary.

Use the large punchneedle for the 4 mm silk ribbon. I suggest you refresh your memory by re-reading Working with Silk Ribbon at the end of Chapter 2, and Silk Ribbons on page 65.

Full-blown flowers

Centres Use the medium needle set at No 3 with the colour indicated on the pattern.

Embroider 20 stitches in a circle (figure 6,

Madeira Decora rayon	Madeira cotton	DMC
pale mauve 1431	*pale mauve 802*	*pale mauve 210*
mid mauve 1432	*purple 804*	*purple 208*
purple 1433	*dark purple 2608*	*dark purple 550*
mid mauve/pink 1521	*pinky mauve 711*	*mauve 554*
dark pink 1588	*pink 707*	*pink 718*
old gold 1470	*light tan 2204*	*light gold 834*

Stitch Glossary). Mark the end of this round to indicate the start of the second round, as seen in figure 6, sample 1, b.

Change to No 2 and work all the way around the initial circle.

Petals These are worked in 2 rows.

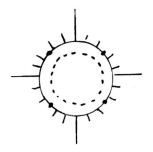

1. Mark circle 2 mm outside first circle
2. Mark circle into quarters
3. Put a dot between each of the 4 marks
4. On either side of each dot put in 2 marks to give 20 points

Positions for 20 silk ribbon loops

Mark 20 dots for the outer circle of loops, 2 mm ($\frac{1}{8}$ in) away from the previous row (see diagram 2).

Punch the full length of the needle, right up to the hilt, to form extra long loops for the outside row of petals. Hold the ribbon loops out of the way on the underside to prevent the needle from punching through the lops already made. Continue until all the large petals are created.

Cut the ribbon and move on to embroider the next beautiful flower.

Half flowers
The two half flowers shown on the pattern are marked X.

Work 10 stitches in a semi-circle with the needle set at No 3, using the rayon thread, then work around the semi circle at No 2.

Work 2 rows of ribbon in a semi-circle, using the technique described above.

Greenery
The small areas of greenery between the flowers are worked with silk ribbon through the large needle set at No 12, working 10 stitches in a circle.

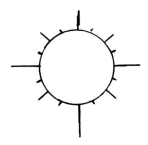

1. Mark circle into quarters
2. Mark between the quarters to make 8 points
3. Mark between the eighths to make 16 points

Positions for 16 silk ribbon loops

With the water-erasable pen, mark 16 points around each flower centre (see diagram 1). Use the large punchneedle set at No 12 for the silk ribbon. Tie a knot in the ribbon where it is pulled through the eye of the needle. The knot prevents the end tag from working its way though to the front of the fabric.

Using the colour ribbon indicated on the pattern, embroider 16 loops around each centre.

Cut the ribbon, but keep the needle threaded.

Remove the casing and spring from the punchneedle, which exposes the full length of the tip (50 mm or 2 inches from the tip to the handle). The needle will still be threaded when removed from the casing.

Tie a knot in the ribbon.

Finishing

Trim all the ends of silk ribbon. Lightly smear craft glue over all the stitching on the back, taking care that the glue is not put onto the surrounding fabric.

Leave to dry.

Heart-shaped frame

Cut the heart shaped frame from a piece of cardboard. Use it as a template to cut two heart-shaped 'frames' of pellon. Put aside the heart-shaped cut-outs from the centres.

Glue the two 'frames' of pellon together, then glue them to the cardboard.

Cut a 23 cm (9 in) square of fabric and place it over the pellon-covered cardboard frame.

Cut around the outside of the heart shape, leaving 15 mm (½ in) fabric as a turnover.

Glue the turnover onto the cardboard. Cut out the fabric in the centre of the heart, leaving the same amount of turnover.

Clip, glue and stretch the inner turnover into position.

Put the frame aside until the cover is made.

Cover

The cover is similar to a dust-jacket for a book. It is made from fabric cut double the height of the album plus 30 mm (1 ¼ in) seam allowance.

Calculate the width required by adding the widths of the front and back plus the width of the spine and adding 50 mm (2 in) to each end.

Fold the fabric in half along its length with wrong sides together.

Stitch along the seam allowance. Press open. Move the seam so that it lies on the back of the fabric casing and halfway between the top and bottom of the album. Turn the fabric right side out.

Cut the embroidery to the heart shape.

Take the two heart-shaped pieces of pellon put aside after cutting the 'frame' pieces, and lightly glue them together. Then glue them to the surface of the album as extra padding behind the ribbon flowers.

Position the embroidered heart on the centre of the front cover over the extra padding. Stitch into place.

Cut a piece of pellon the same width and length as the back, front and spine. Place this inside the fabric casing, adding padding to the fabric cover.

Neaten the two ends of the cover.

Place the fabric casing over the album and turn in the ends to fit. Hand-stitch in place.

Place the covered heart-shaped frame over the ribbon embroidery, releasing any loops which may become trapped.

Lift the edge of the frame and glue underneath, working carefully around the frame to prevent glue getting onto the ribbon. (If you glue the back of the frame before putting it in position, you risk getting glue on the ribbons.)

Leave to dry.

Now there, you are the proud owner of a beautifully covered album.

It is such a lovely thing to keep and treasure. It is also a gorgeous, relatively easy to make gift for a friend—a particularly delightful wedding present.

You can surround the heart-shaped frame with a braid if you wish. Use six strands of each of the colours used in the centre of the flowers (see Braid Making in Stitch Glossary).

15 MAGICAL MINIATURE CARPET

Gently embroider this colourful, magical masterpiece as a treasured miniature to enjoy and keep forever.

In excess of 28 metres (over 30 yards) of one strand of embroidery thread is used in each of these little miniatures, each approximately 4.2 cm (1 ⅝ in) square.

I have worked approximately 435 stitched loops per square centimetre.

Materials

any very fine punchneedle which uses only one strand of thread, such as the Delite or Igolochkoy™ punchneedles

15 cm (6 in) lip-lock hoop

20 cm (8 in) square of tightly woven fabric

sharp embroidery scissors

very fine steel crochet hook

You Can Wash It craft glue

very fine, sharp lead pencil or 0.1 Unipen

small piece of plastic tubing

Embroidery threads

Madeira	DMC
pink 603	*pink 3350*
black 2400	*black 310*
dark blue 1007	*dark blue 336*
blue 906	*blue 793*

Plus variegated thread No 109 blue bayou from Necessity Notions in colours through white and grey to pale blue and medium blue-grey.

Preparation

Place the fabric in the hoop, ensuring that it is taut and the hoop nut is done up very tightly.

It is important with this piece of embroidery that the design is traced absolutely straight onto the fabric. The way to do this is to mark the straight grain of the fabric (see Chapter 4).

Using diagram 3 as the tracing pattern, mark the required length for one side of the miniature along the warp of the fabric with tiny dots and then, using pressure from the back of the crochet hook, score a line between the dots. Measure a second side at right angles along the weft of the fabric and mark with a dot. Score with the crochet hook. Measure for the other two sides and score the lines to achieve the required square shape. The lines may look a little distorted when the fabric is stretched so tightly in the hoop, but

when the finished embroidery is removed from the hoop it can be stretched into a perfect square.

Mark over the scored lines lightly with a fine pen. Remove the fabric from the hoop so that the design can be traced squarely onto the fabric within the scored lines. Position the design underneath the scored lines on the fabric and trace onto the back of the fabric using your preferred transferring technique. For this design a fine outline is essential. Use either a very well-sharpened lead pencil or a 0.1 Unipen or Micron pen.

Embroidery

TIP

To work this design with the very fine punchneedle, set the needle length at 6 mm (¼ in) from the eye of the needle to the handle. If you have trouble keeping the loops in place, increase the length. If the needle tip is too short, the loops cannot stay in place. Remember that the thickness of the fabric you are using takes up some length of the loop.

For this piece I have worked into every space between the fibres of the fabric.

With the stitches very close together, work the black outline of the square.

Work black along the lines within the design.

Fill in the colours as shown in diagram 4.

Finishing

Check the completed piece to see that the loops on the front are all even. Use the crochet hook to carefully pull any longer loops through to the back. With the crochet hook, score the fabric 10 mm (about ½ in) from the two ends which will be fringed.

Remove the fabric from the hoop and pull into shape.

Trim the ends of the threads on the back, very close to the surface. Smear You Can Wash It craft glue over the entire back of the embroidery,

How to draw a design?

Many of my students tell me that they are unable to come up with their own design ideas. I was in that same position some years ago and once I was shown the method I am about to describe, my whole creative world changed. I have a very talented Australian embroiderer to thank for this gem. My other suggestion, if you feel that you are not good with colour choice, is to look around at what colours other artists have put together and be guided by their choices.

One can take inspiration from other artists without directly copying their work. Artists who design wrapping paper, for example, have the training to produce effective design and colour combinations. Benefit from their skill and interpret their ideas into your own work. There is nothing more satisfying than to know that you have developed your own design, albeit with a little help from talented designers.

By following this method you can achieve designs that you never imagined possible.

Any design, looked upon through a small viewfinder, changes in its presentation dramatically. You can break a design down to its minimum elements to create something vastly different from what you first saw.

A simple method of minimising the elements of any design is to cut a 2.5 cm (1 in) square hole from a piece of paper or cardboard (a simple viewfinder). Place this square frame over, for example, a piece of wrapping paper and move it slowly over the paper, observing the mini designs captured in the frame. When the frame rests on an area that is pleasing to your eye, tape it in position (see diagram 2a).

Diagram 1: Large design area

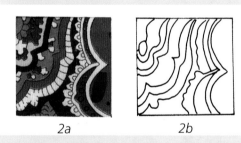

2a   *2b*

Diagram 2: Area selected in viewfinder and copied

Diagram 3: Design enlarged and simplified for tracing

PUNCHNEEDLE EMBROIDERY — DANCING NEEDLES

Place tracing paper over the frame and draw the design captured in the square. Do not draw everything you can see, but minimise the number of lines (see diagram 2b).

For my miniature I enlarged the tiny square drawing to nearly one and a half times the size. Look at your enlarged drawing and add or subtract various elements to come up with a pleasing final result which becomes your tracing pattern (diagram 3).

Colour key

- pink 603
- variegated 109
- dark blue 1007
- blue 906
- black

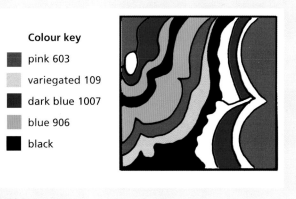

Diagram 4

Colour in the drawing with pencils or paint, either attempting to match the original paper or substituting colours of your own (diagram 4). Colouring in your drawing gives a huge sense of accomplishment.

Choose threads to match the colours of your final piece of artwork.

taking care to keep the glue away from the areas where the thread will be drawn to make the fringes. Leave to dry.

Carefully cut the completed miniature away from the fabric, close to the two sides and along the scored lines at the ends where the fringes will be made.

Fray the fibres to make the fringes, leaving 2 or 3 fibres in place next to the embroidery.

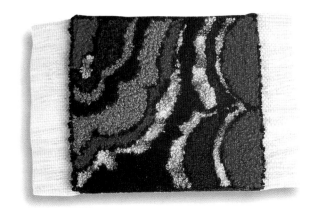

TIP

There is a lovely miniature worked in punchneedle embroidery in the Craft Artists Ornaments at the American White House. It is featured on the Internet at: http://clinton4.nara.gov/WH/Holidays/1999/ornamentscraft2.html
It states that there are approximately 1200 individual loops and stitches per square inch.

16 A GRAND OLD PEDESTAL

A pedestal and urn, brimming with fragrant pansies, stands regally, partly hidden among bright nasturtiums flowing over weathered cobblestones. The version in the photograph is worked in Madeira cottons.

Materials

25 cm (10 in) hoop
35 cm (14 in) square of fabric
sharp embroidery scissors
small and medium punchneedles
2 mm piece of plastic tubing
2 flat-backed terracotta pots, approx. 2 x 1.5 cm
   (¾ x ½ in)

small piece of double-sided tape
You Can Wash It craft glue
Water-erasable pen/fine lead pencil
Pentel Hybrid Roller (grey pen) or Fabrico pen in
   cool grey (if not available use preferred fabric
   colouring technique)

**Tracing pattern for
A Grand Old Urn**

actual size

Stitch guide

See colour photograph for placement of colour

Key

- • pale mauve 801
- ⊙ pale pink 2712
- ⊗ very dark purple 2608

- ✹ pale yellow 102
- ✸ orange 206
- ▬ red 211
- ⊕ yellow 107

Threads

Embroidery cotton

Madeira	DMC
green 1502	green 470
green 1503	green 469
green 1504	green 937
dark purple 2608	dark purple 550
mauve 801	mauve 211
light pink 2712	light pink 963
pale yellow 102	pale yellow 3078
yellow 107	yellow 972
orange 206	orange 946
red 211	red 817
brown 1911	brown 841
grey 1813	grey 647

Traditional punchneedle embroidery acrylic yarn

Some acrylic yarn colours listed are quite different to the Madeira colours in the photograph, and also differ noticeably between the two brands. I have chosen colours that work well together.

Cameo	Pretty Punch
aspen green 25	aspen green 67
dark aspen 26	dark aspen 68
avocado 69	medium avocado 69
light lavender 36	dark lavender 8
orchid 4	orchid 9
pink 20	raspberry 6
baby yellow 43	baby maize 19
gold yellow 45	bright lemon 55
burnt orange 73	bright orange 73
deep red 86	poinsettia red 62
tan 55	medium sand 33
light grey 63	silver grey 75

Preparation

Check the straight grain of the fabric.

Use a light-box or well-lit window to make the tracing process easier, and align the design with the warp of the fabric, straight up and down.

With the Pentel pen, carefully trace the outline of the urn and pedestal onto the front of the fabric.

Trace the spiky grasses at the base of the design onto the front of the fabric with the water-erasable pen. Trace the remainder of the design onto the back of fabric using your preferred method of tracing.

Place the fabric tightly in the hoop with the tracing of the urn uppermost.

Shade colour with the Pentel pen into the outlined area of the urn and pedestal. Leave some areas lighter than others (see photograph). As the ink dries it may be necessary to add more colour to achieve a satisfactory depth of colour.

Embroidery

This design uses three strands of embroidery cotton through the small punchneedle and six strands through the medium punchneedle.

The acrylic yarn is used in the medium punchneedle.

The instructions are for working in Madeira threads. Substitute if working in one of the other threads.

Urn and pedestal

Outline with reverse punchneedle embroidery (figure 7, a, Stitch Glossary) following the lines indicated on the pattern, with three strands of grey 1813 at No 1. Pull the start and finish ends through to the back.

Spiky grasses

Stitch the three tufts of spiky grasses at the foot of the urn and at the front of the design in backward reverse punchneedle embroidery (see Figure 7, f, Stitch Glossary), using a combination of the three greens 1502, 1503 and 1504 to add interest.

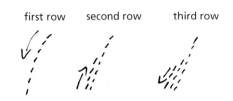

Diagram 1: Green spikes in urn

Remove the fabric from the hoop, turn it over, and replace it tightly with the back of the design uppermost.

Use the small punchneedle with three strands of thread unless stated.

Green spikes in urn

With the 2 mm piece of plastic tubing (see Pile Depth) on the small needle set at No 1, work the spikes in green 1504. Using the plastic is optional here, but it does give a finer finish to the embroidery as the loops are shorter.

TIP

When punching the very tip of the spike, angle the needle into the centre at about 20–30 degrees (see figure 10, Stitch Glossary). This seats the tip down. If you work this loop in the usual way, it will sit up straight and look raggedy.

Start embroidering each spike from the tip. Angle the needle at the beginning of the first row and work in to the centre. Work the second row backwards and very close to the first row, ending 3 stitches below the tip. Begin the third row 1 stitch below the second row and work forward into the centre (see diagram 1). Working in this manner creates a finer tip.

Pansies in urn

Follow the colour placement on the stitch guide. Set the needle at No 2. Work each flower with 8 stitches in a circle (figure 6, sample 1, Stitch Glossary).

Greenery in urn

With the needle set at No 1, take one strand each of greens 1502, 1503 and 1504 and thread all together through the needle to fill in the greenery around and among the pansies. Work from the back in normal punchneedle embroidery.

Nasturtiums and greenery overflowing from urn

Use yellow 107, orange 206 and green 1503. The flowers and greenery toward the top are worked at No 1 with 5 or 6 stitches in a circle. Toward the bottom of the overflowing trail, shorten the punchneedle tip with the 2 mm piece of plastic tubing. Embroider the greenery and then intermingle the flowers, placing 2 or 3 stitches only to make up the flowers (see main stitch guide and photograph).

Pansies in terracotta pots

Mark a line along the tops of the pots on the fabric as a guide for placing the flowers, and follow the pattern. As the needle can be damaged if it scrapes the terracotta pots, it is better that

Stitch guide for nasturtiums

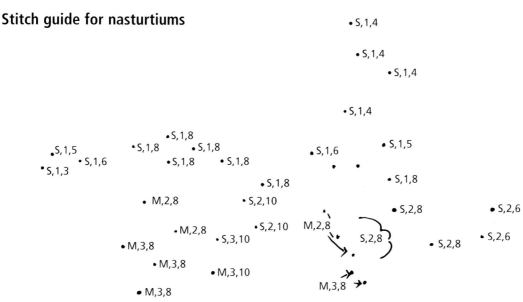

Examples:

S, 1, 10 = small needle at No 1, with 10 stitches in circle

M, 3, 8 = medium needle at No 3, with 8 stitches in circle

they are not glued in position at this stage. (If you want to get an idea of how your embroidery is progressing, you can temporarily stick the pots in position with the double-sided tape, but remember to remove them again.)

Cobblestones

The four cobblestones in the foreground are worked with the medium needle set at No 2 with three strands of brown 1911 and three strands of grey 1813 together in the medium needle.

The smaller cobblestones are worked with two strands of brown 1911 and one strand of grey 1813 together in the small needle set at No 1. Cut some of the loops on these stones to alter the colour and texture.

Nasturtiums between cobblestones

I actually sat in my nasturtium patch, colour chart in hand, to choose these colours and those for the pansies. I was amazed at the closeness in colour

between the nasturtium flowers and the embroidery thread.

Follow the stitch guide for the nasturtiums to put in the yellows, reds and oranges, observing the needle changes required. For example: S, 1, 10 means: use the small needle set at No 1 and work 10 stitches in a circle. Use three strands in the small needle, six strands in the medium needle.

Grass around terracotta pots

For the area under the pots, start the stitching 3 mm (⅛ in) below the pot. Punch in 9 loops at No 9 in the medium needle, using green 1503. Turn the embroidery over, and on the front work reverse punchneedle embroidery across the base of the loops. This stitching keeps the tufts standing upright. Some of the tufts in the foreground on the left are worked with the needle set at No 9 and some at No 12. Cut the loops to varying lengths to resemble a grassy tuft.

**Colour guide for green leaves
between nasturtiums and
cobblestones**

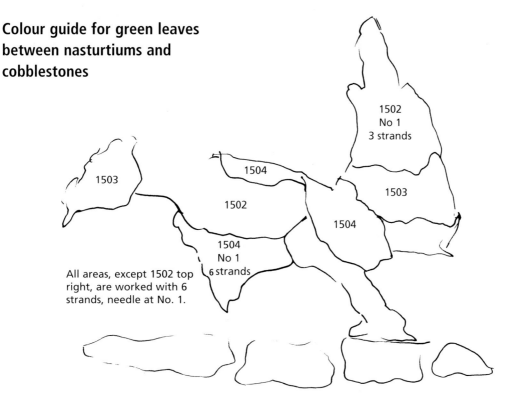

1502
No 1
3 strands

1503

1504

1502

1503

1504

1504
No 1
6 strands

All areas, except 1502 top
right, are worked with 6
strands, needle at No. 1.

Between the cobblestones use 1503 and 1504 randomly, at No 1 and No 2

For the area on the right, set the needle at No 12 and pull the thread from the needle under the fabric, at the front, so that some loops are much longer. Trim these to 30 mm (1 ¼ in).

Grass between the cobblestones

Use greens 1503 and 1504 to work at No 1 and No 2. Trim some of the loops, particularly in the foreground, so that the texture becomes velvety and moss-like. The trimmed loops change to a deeper colour, adding extra interest to the foreground.

Green leaves between the nasturtiums

Follow the colour guide for the placement of the three greens between the nasturtiums and the cobblestones.

Finishing

Remove fabric from hoop and stretch in all directions to straighten the embroidery.

Glue the pots carefully in position, lifting the loops away so no glue gets on them, and allow to dry.

Trim any long ends from the back, and press around the embroidery.

Cut pellon or wadding to fit underneath, frame your embroidery and enjoy it!

17 LILY AND HYACINTHS

A wonderful weathered pot full of gentle grape hyacinths, wispy orchid leaves and a very precious white lily. Errant hyacinths share the base with scattered stones surrounded by cool green moss. The framed embroidery is worked in Madeira cotton, the embroidery in the closeup in Cameo acrylic yarn.

Tracing pattern for Lily and Hyacinths
actual size

Materials

15 and 20 cm (6 and 8 in) lip-lock hoops
20 and 25 cm (8 and 10 in) squares of fabric
sharp embroidery scissors
small, medium and large punchneedles
2 mm piece of plastic tubing
15 cm (6 in) of 28 gauge wire
sewing needle
Nymo thread
flat-backed terracotta pot, 8 x 4 cm (3 x 1 ½ in)
small piece of double-sided tape
You Can Wash It craft glue
water-erasable pen /fine lead pencil
Jo Sonja paints: teal green, rich gold (optional)
gold artificial stamens (optional)
small flat pebbles

Threads

Embroidery cotton

Madeira	DMC
green 1509	*green 3052*
green 1504	*green 937*
green 1502	*green 470*
purple 714	*purple 550*
mauve 802	*mauve 210*
mauve 803	*mauve 219*
white	*white*
(optional) Bunka rayon thread, greens 172 and 173	

Traditional punchneedle embroidery acrylic yarn

The colour conversion from one acrylic yarn to another is not always exact. I have chosen colours that work well together.

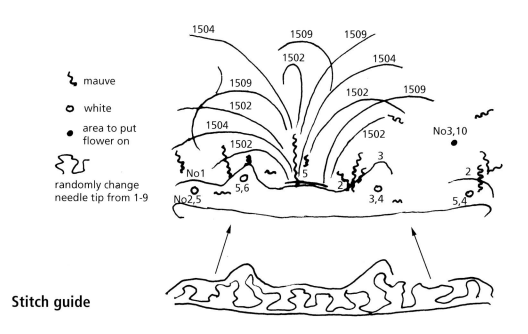

Stitch guide

Cameo	Pretty Punch
aspen green 25	*aspen green 67*
dark aspen 26	*dark green 68*
avocado 69	*medium avocado 69*
light lavender 36	*dark lavender 8*
orchid 4	*orchid 9*
white	*white*

Preparation

If desired, paint some colour onto the 25 cm (10 in) square of background fabric or use a Rainbow transfer paper (see Chapter 4), positioning it so that the design will be drawn on the green area.

You may choose to paint the terracotta pot. Dab on some Jo Sonja teal green paint and rub in gently. When dry, rub a small quantity of rich gold paint over the top, leaving some terracotta colour showing through.

Mark the position of the top of the terracotta pot on both front and back of the larger piece of fabric with the water-erasable pen or fine lead pencil. Mark the position for the bottom of the pot on the straight grain of the fabric.

Trace the lines for the fine orchid-like leaves onto the front of the fabric with a water erasable pen or a very fine lead pencil. Trace the remainder of the design onto the back. (The smaller square of fabric is used for the free-standing lily.)

Place the fabric in the 20 cm (8 in) hoop with the tracing of the orchid-like leaves uppermost. (These leaves are worked first, on the front of the fabric.) You may wish to use a doughnut to protect the fabric.

Stick the double-sided tape to the back of the terracotta pot. If you want to get an idea of how your embroidery is progressing, you can temporarily stick the pot in position with the double-sided tape, but remember to remove it again. Take care when turning the work over, as the tape may not hold strongly enough to prevent the pot falling off and becoming damaged if it hits a hard surface. Resist the temptation to glue the pot in place before the embroidery is finished, as it is very easy to scrape the needle along the pot as you work, causing damage to both.

Embroidery

The following instructions refer to Madeira colours. Substitute if using another thread.

TIP

When using acrylic thread, set the punchneedle two settings higher than in these instructions, except for the reverse punchneedle embroidery, which is worked at No 1.

Grassy leaves

Use the small needle set at No 1 and three strands of greens 1502, 1504 and 1509 as indicated on the stitch guide. The use of the small piece of plastic tubing to shorten the loops is optional (see Pile Depth). Using the backward reverse punchneedle embroidery technique (figure 7, f, Stitch Glossary), commence at the bottom of each spike. Pull the starting and ending threads through to the back of the fabric, where they are trimmed and can be given a smear of glue to prevent them working their way onto the front.

Remove the fabric from the hoop, turn it over and replace the fabric tightly into the hoop with the back of fabric uppermost.

Other greenery

Change to the medium punchneedle. Take 2 strands each of greens 1502, 1504 and 1509 and put them together. (If using acrylic yarn, thread all three greens through the large punchneedle.) Stitch along the line drawn for the top of the pot, following the stitch guide to vary the length of the loops.

Using the same greens, stitch along the undulating line running under the grassy leaves. Change the length of the needle tip between Nos 1, 2 and 3 as shown on the stitch guide, and directly under the spikes use No 5.

Remember to carefully keep turning the piece over to see the overall effect on the front of the fabric.

With one of the greens, make a circle with 10 stitches at No 3, on the marked dot (for both types of thread). The lily flower is placed on this small raised circle later.

Fill in the area between the top of the pot and the undulating line with meandering stitch, randomly changing the length of the loops between Nos 1 and 9. Avoid creating the appearance of straight rows (see figure 9, Stitch Glossary). (As acrylic thread fills in thickly, leave a few small spaces so that the area does not become overfull.) Allow the loops to group together along the top so that there is no definite outline.

Small white flowers

Use the medium needle to work the small white flowers with six strands of cotton on the four open circles, following stitch lengths and number of stitches as marked on the stitch guide. (If using acrylic yarn, work each area at No 5 with one thickness in the medium punchneedle.)

Grape hyacinths

These are worked with two strands each of purple 714, and mauves 802 and 803 together in the medium needle. (If using acrylic yarn, put the two mauves together in the large punchneedle.) Work the stitching along the squiggly lines on the stitch guide. Work downwards from the top of each line, starting with 2 stitches at No 1 at the top, then changing to No 2 and working to the length required.

Look at the photograph and work out where to put in any extra fill-in colour in mauve and white.

Add a few small groups of fallen flowers in mauve at the base of the pot, following the photograph.

At this point, if you have not been able to acquire the Bunka thread, embroider some loops of green at varying lengths from No 1 to No 5 around and under the terracotta pot, following the photo for placement and using two strands of each green in the medium needle. (If using acrylic yarn, use the three green colours together in the large punchneedle.) If you do have the Bunka thread, leave this section of greenery till later.

Free-standing lily

Trace the outline of the lily onto the back of the 20 cm (8 in) square of fabric with a water-erasable pen.

Place the fabric very taut in the 15 cm (6 in) hoop and do up the nut very tightly.

With the sewing needle and Nymo thread (used for stitching beads), overstitch in the centre of the flower to secure the thread.

Tracing pattern and stitch guide for free-standing lily

pattern

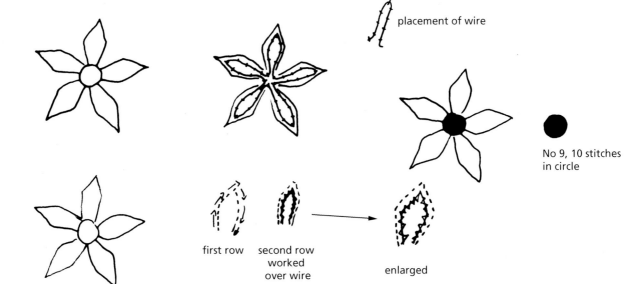

placement of wire

No 9, 10 stitches in circle

first row   second row worked over wire   enlarged

Lay the wire over the fabric, securing the end with an oversew or couching stitch at the centre. Manipulate the wire up one side of a petal, just inside the outline, couching it down as you go (see diagram).

To change direction at the tip of the petal, bring the sewing needle up from the front of the fabric inside the wire, pull the thread tight and, using it for leverage, pull the wire around in a gentle curve and couch it down the other side of the petal.

At the centre, where the wire needs to be turned up to go along the next petal, again use the thread to help turn the wire. If the thread isn't strong enough, bend the wire around the needle.

Continue around all petals in this manner.

Cut the ends of the wire very close to the fabric with an old pair of scissors or cutters, pressing both ends down firmly with the point of the scissors so that they lie very close to the surface of the fabric.

Use the small needle at No 1 with three strands of white cotton (one thread of acrylic). Starting from the centre, stitch along the outline of a petal with very small stitches, working all the way around the petal back to the centre. At the tip of the petal it is important to angle the needle into the centre to prevent an overhanging loop (see Figure 10, Stitch Glossary). The next row of stitching, inside the first, is worked over the wire in a zigzag fashion (see diagram).

Back at the centre, work some small stitches across to the next petal and start again. Continue until all petals are stitched.

Work the centre with the small needle at No 9 with 20 stitches in a circle with three strands of yellow (one thickness of acrylic).

Cut the loops of the centre to approximately 6 mm (¼ in) above the fabric. Cutting the loops gives a fluffy appearance.

If original stamens are not available, from the back work 5 stitches through the yellow centre with yellow thread at No 9 and cut the loops open. Stiffen the threads with a small amount of glue.

Remove the fabric from the hoop and stretch it in all directions to straighten out the embroidery.

Glue over the back of the flower, using your index finger to rub the glue into the fabric along the outline row of stitching. Leave to dry.

With very sharp scissors carefully cut the flower away from the fabric. If some of the outside loops need to be cut to give more shape to the petals, use a smear of glue to seal the edges.

To sharpen the petal tips, rub a little glue between thumb and index finger and place it on either side of the tip.

If using artificial stamens, cut them to 6 mm (¼ in) long, dip the cut ends in glue and position the stamens in a circle in the yellow centre. Manipulate the finished flower into a gentle saucer-shaped curve.

Finishing

Remove the larger square of fabric from the hoop and stretch it in all directions to straighten out the embroidery.

Glue the terracotta pot into position.

With a little glue on the back of the flower, place it on the dot worked in green, sitting it at an angle rather than absolutely straight-on, and leave to dry.

Glue a few small flat pebbles under and around the pot.

This is where the Bunka thread is used. It comes in a round knitted tube. When pulled, it unravels and becomes crinkly. Take a length, grasp it at the very tips, then pull it so that it becomes much longer, finer, drawn-out and crinkly. Let the crinkly thread fall gently over the base and glue it into position with a very little glue, over the pot and in and around the pebbles, to resemble moss.

Press the outside edges of the embroidery to remove any marks left by the hoop.

Place two layers of pellon under the embroidery prior to framing in a box frame.

18 CREAM ON CREAM

*This dainty cream stitching on an elegant cream cushion is embroidered in
Madeira 2-ply candlewick thread.*

Tracing pattern for Cream on Cream
enlarge at 108%

Stitch guide

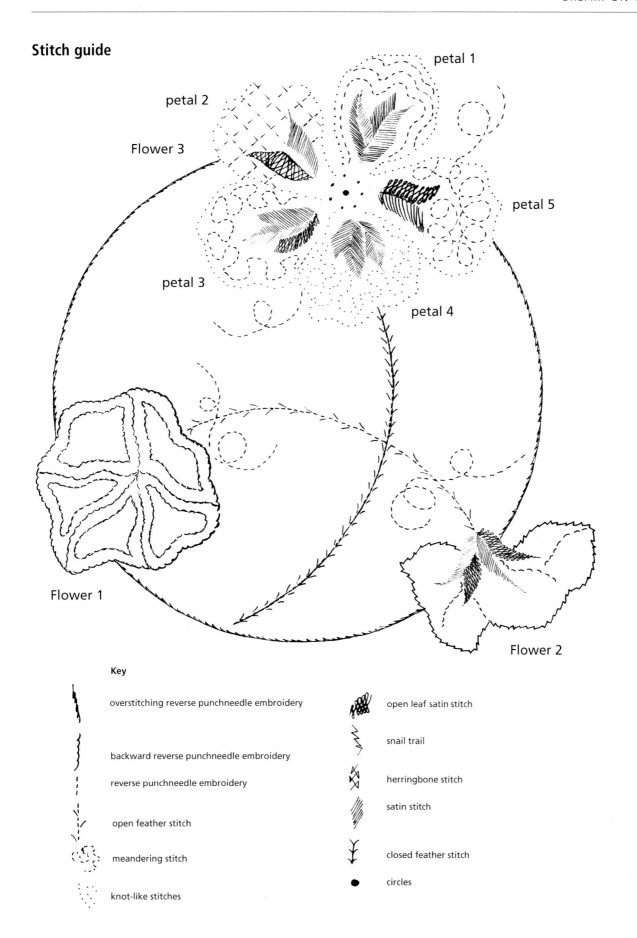

petal 1

petal 2

Flower 3

petal 5

petal 3

petal 4

Flower 1

Flower 2

Key

overstitching reverse punchneedle embroidery

backward reverse punchneedle embroidery

reverse punchneedle embroidery

open feather stitch

meandering stitch

knot-like stitches

open leaf satin stitch

snail trail

herringbone stitch

satin stitch

closed feather stitch

circles

Materials

small punchneedle
25 cm (10 in) lip-lock hoop
30 cm (12 in) square of tightly woven fabric
sharp embroidery scissors
2 mm piece of plastic tubing
You Can Wash It craft glue
water-erasable pen
fine lead pencil
fine steel crochet hook

Thread

Madeira cream 2-ply candlewick thread (or
*   similar).*

Traditional candlewick designs are worked with an embroidery needle and thread in a variety of stitches, although the main stitch used is the colonial knot. This candlewick look-alike punch embroidery is mainly worked with surface stitches on the front of the fabric. Only a very small area is worked from the back in the traditional manner.

Preparation

Photocopy the design at 108% and trace onto the front of the fabric. Use a water-erasable pen so that any outline not fully covered by embroidery may be sponged away. It is important to remember that the markings from this pen can fade, quite quickly at times. As a precaution, if the embroidery is not going to be worked straightaway, lightly trace the design onto the back of the fabric as well with a soft lead pencil (not an iron-on pen). Then, as the design fades from the front it can be re-traced from the outline on the back.

Embroidery

The placements of the various stitches used in this design are indicated on the stitch guide.

Follow the stitch guide on the pattern sheet.

This design is all worked with the small punchneedle with the needle set at No 1 except where satin stitch is being worked, when the needle will need to be set at No 2. Please note if the loop is not staying in place on the back increase the length of the needle tip.

Flower 1

This flower is worked entirely in backward reverse punchneedle embroidery (figure 7, sample f, Stitch Glossary).

Flower 2

The outline is worked in snail trail (figure 7, sample e, Stitch Glossary).

The lines dividing the petals are worked in reverse punchneedle embroidery.

The centre areas are worked in open leaf stich and satin stitch as indicated on the pattern sheet.

Flower 3

This flower is mostly worked from the front with various surface stitches.

The outer edges are worked from the back in knot-like stitch (figure 21, a, Stitch Glossary). A 2 mm piece of plastic is placed on the needle tip (see Pile Depth) to shorten the loop on the front when working the knot-like stitches so that the loops look more like tiny knots than loops.

Centre With the 2mm plastic on the needle set at No 1 work the centre with 8 stitches in a circle (figure 6, sample 1, a, Stitch Glossary). The smaller circles are worked with 4 stitches in a circle.

Petal 1 Outer section is worked in reverse punchneedle embroidery (figure 7, sample a, Stitch Glossary); the inner section is worked in satin stitch (figure 7, h, Stitch Glossary) and leaf stitch (figure 8, Stitch Glossary).

Petal 2 The crosshatching is worked in reverse punchneedle embroidery.

The inner section has half of the area worked in satin stitch and the other in open leaf stitch (figure 7, sample k, Stitch Glossary).

Petal 3 The meandering stitch is worked in reverse punchneedle embroidery. The inner section is worked in satin stitch and open leaf stitch.

Petal 4 The area which looks like little knots is worked in knot stitch (figure 21, b, Stitch Glossary), working the stitching in a meandering way with a 2 mm piece of plastic placed on the needle tip.

The inner section is worked in satin stitch and leaf stitch.

Petal 5 The swirling lines are worked in reverse punchneedle embroidery.

The inner section is worked in satin stitch and open leaf stitch.

Connecting circle

The circle is worked in backward reverse punchneedle embroidery.

The two inner curved lines

Follow the pattern sheet as a guide. One line is worked with closed feather stitch (figure 7, sample b, Stitch Glossary) and the other in open feather stitch (figure 7, sample c, Stitch Glossary).

The tendrils

These are worked in reverse punchneedle embroidery.

Finishing

This stunning cream design can be framed or made into a cushion. A quilt top worked in pretend candlewick squares also looks sensational when pieced together. It is important to remember, however, that because the loops have not been worked closely together they may not stay in place when washed, or stand up to the wear and tear that a cushion might normally be subjected to.

If the completed piece is intended for anything other than framing, smear the stitching on the back with You Can Wash It craft glue, taking care to put the glue *only on the stitching* and not the surrounding fabric. Gluing from the back in this manner reinforces the embroidery to withstand normal wear and tear and gentle laundering.

19 CIRCLE UPON A CIRCLE

*These circles of love and completeness gently hold an astonishing selection of
colourful flowers, leaves and beautiful stitches. This embroidery is worked in
Rajmahal art silk.*

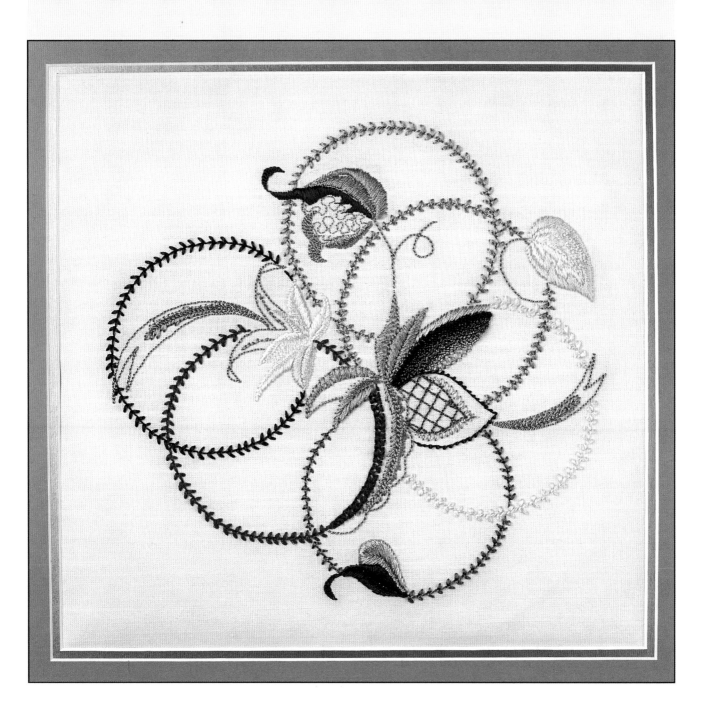

Tracing pattern for Circle Upon a Circle
enlarge at 140%

Stitch guide

Key

satin stitch

backwards reverse
punchneedle embroidery

snail trail, very close together

reverse punchneedle embroidery

open leaf satin stitch

open leaf stain stitch with
reverse punchneedle embroidery
worked through the centre

snail trail

herringbone stitch

meandering stitch

closed feather stitch

zigzag stitch

Materials

medium punchneedle

25 cm (10 in) lip-lock hoop

35 cm (14 in) square of fabric

sharp embroidery scissors

Fray Stop

You Can Wash It craft glue

water-erasable pen

fine steel crochet hook

fabric doughnut

Threads

Rajmahal art silks

maidenhair 521

green earth 421

dainty lilac 111

purple dusk 113

imperial purple 115

bluebell 121

gentle magenta 181

vibrant musk 184

winter white 90

wheat gold 91

moroccan gold 94

Preparation

Photocopy the design at 140% and trace onto the front of the fabric with the water-erasable pen. Any outline which is not fully covered by the embroidery can later be sponged away. Remember that the markings from this pen can fade, quite quickly at times, so if the embroidery is not going to be worked straightaway, lightly trace the design onto the back of the fabric as well with a soft lead pencil. Then, as the design fades from the front, it can be retraced from the outline on the back.

It is a good idea to cut a 10 cm (3 ⅞ in) circle from cardboard, clear acetate or plastic to use as a template. If the circles become a little distorted when the fabric is tightened in the hoop, use the template over each circle as a guide to help pull it back into shape while you are embroidering it.

I highly recommend the use of a doughnut when embroidering this piece. As most of the embroidery is done on the front, the edges may easily become soiled.

Embroidery

This is a very delicate piece of embroidery worked almost entirely from the front using various reverse punchneedle embroidery stitches. There is very little normal punchneedle embroidery in this beautiful piece.

Follow the stitch guide and colour placement on the pattern, re-reading the Stitch Glossary if necessary to refresh your memory.

For the areas worked in satin stitch, follow the stitch guide for the direction of stitching and use the needle set at No 2. If the loops will not stay in place on the back of the embroidery, increase the needle length (see Pile Depth).

TIPS

The Rajmahal thread is shiny and slippery. The medium needle can leave an opening between the fibres of the fabric through which the ends of the shiny thread can slip to the front. This can to some extent be 'fixed' by closing the fibres together by scratching the back of the fabric with a finger tip. Where the slipping of thread is a problem treat the end of the thread on the back of the piece with a small amount of Fray Stop or You Can Wash It craft glue. Take care that the glue does not seep through to the front of the fabric

A small knot tied at the end of the thread after threading the needle will hold the beginning thread in place and prevent some threads from working their way to the front of the fabric. Remember, though, where you are working reverse punchneedle embroidery you will need to push the needle through the fabric, take the end tag of thread to the back of the fabric and then tie the knot.

**Colour guide for
Rajmahal threads**

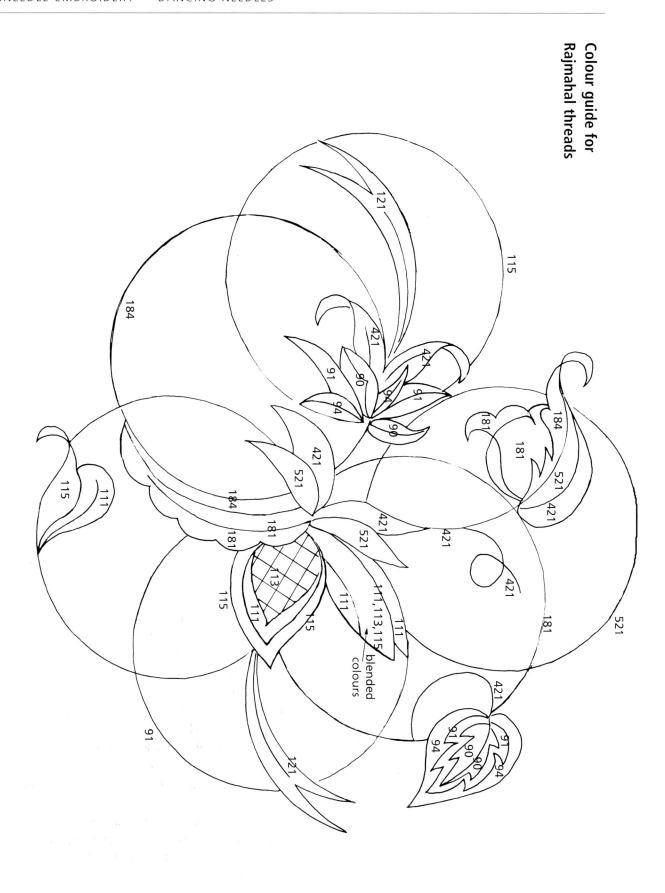

Blended colour area

The one small area of normal punchneedle embroidery in the centre of the design is worked with blended threads using mauves 111 and 113, and purple 115. Blending threads together gives subtle colour changes (see figure 17, Stitch Glossary).

Working from the outside in:

Work 2 rows with 6 strands of dark purple at No 1.

Take 4 strands of dark purple and 2 strands of mid mauve and thread them together through the needle. Work 2 rows at No 2.

Take 4 strands of mid mauve and 2 strands of dark purple. Work 2 rows at No 3.

Take 6 strands of mid mauve and work 2 rows at No 3.

Take 4 strands of mid mauve and 2 strands of pale mauve. Work 2 rows at No 2.

Take 4 strands of pale mauve and 2 strands of mid mauve. Work 2 rows at No 2.

For the last 2 rows use 6 strands of pale mauve at No 1.

If a small area remains empty after this, fill it with the pale mauve at No 1.

Leaf 1

Use colours green earth 421, maidenhair 521, vibrant musk 184 and gentle magenta 181, and work satin stitch.

The meandering reverse punchneedle embroidery (figure 9, Stitch Glossary) is worked in gentle magenta 181.

The longest tip of the leaf is worked with reverse punchneedle embroidery (figure 7, a, Stitch Glossary) very close together with vibrant musk 184.

The shorter tip is worked in the above manner with gentle magenta 181.

Leaf 2

This is worked in varying shades of yellow—moroccan gold 94, wheat gold 91 and winter white 90.

Work in satin stitch (figure 7, h and i, Stitch Glossary). Follow the stitch guide for the angle to work the satin stitch, and the colour guide for colour placement.

Leaf 3

This is worked with bluebell 121, the outer edges in reverse punchneedle embroidery and the centre in open leaf stitch with reverse punchneedle embroidery (figure 7, l, Stitch Glossary).

Leaf 4

Use dainty lilac 111 and imperial purple 115. Follow the stitch guide for the angle to work the satin stitch, and the colour guide for colour placement.

Leaf 5

Use winter white 90, moroccan gold 94, wheat gold 91 and green earth 421. Follow the stitch guide for the angle to work the satin stitch, and the colour guide for colour placement. There is an area worked in open leaf stitch (figure 7, k, Stitch Glossary).

Two short lines of snail trail (figure 7, e, Stitch Glossary) are embroidered for the veins.

Leaf 6

Work in bluebell 121 in the same manner as Leaf 3.

Centre leaves

a Use green earth 421 and herringbone stitch (figure 7, Stitch Glossary). Glue the ends of the threads on the back of the work.

b Use maidenhair 521 in open leaf stitch.

c Use dainty lilac 111 in satin stitch.

d Blended colour area. See instructions, page 171.

e Use dainty lilac 111 in herringbone stitch.

f The outside edge is worked in snail trail with imperial purple 115. Work the zigzag stitch (figure 22, Stitch Glossary) in dainty lilac 111. Work the cross hatching in reverse punchneedle embroidery in purple dusk 113.

g Use gentle magenta 181 with open leaf satin stitch with reverse punchneedle embroidery and outline the area in reverse punchneedle embroidery.

h Use herringbone stitch in vibrant musk 184.

i Use maidenhair 521 in satin stitch.

j Work in green earth 421 in herringbone stitch and backwards reverse punchneedle embroidery (figure 7, f, Stitch Glossary).

Circles

The circle outlines are all worked in closed feather stitch (figure 7, b, Stitch Glossary). Use the colours indicated on the colour chart.

Stems

Work in reverse punchneedle embroidery with green earth 421.

Finishing

Remove the fabric from the hoop and stretch it in all directions to straighten the embroidery.

Press around the embroidery carefully to remove any marks left by the hoop, and place a double layer of pellon under the piece prior to framing it.

20 A PROMISE OF SUMMER

A bright and beautiful mass of yellow flowers, a reminder that summer is just around the corner. This piece is worked in glossy, shining silk ribbons.

Materials

Dancing Ribbon needle

25 cm (10 in) hoop

2 x 35 cm (14 in) fabric squares

iron-on woven interfacing (optional)

45 x 30 cm (18 x 12 in) coloured fabric (to arrange under urn)

flat-backed ceramic urn, approx. 8 x 6 cm (3 x 2 ¼ in)

water-erasable pen

You Can Wash It craft glue

sewing needle and thread

small quantity of soft wadding

Ribbons

13 mm (approx. ½ in) Kakoonda silk ribbon: yellow 103, mauve 3C

7 mm (just over ¼ in) Kakoonda silk ribbon: yellow 103, green 306

13 mm (approx. ½ in) Hannah bias-cut silk ribbon: variegated green

Stunning flowers are made when embroidering with the Dancing Ribbon Needle. However, this technique does use 'lots' of ribbon, about 2.5 metres (approximately 100 inches) for each of the big flowers. It is definitely worth it!!

Introducing the Dancing Ribbon needle— the needle that really dances!

The results achieved from embroidering with the Dancing Ribbon Needle are exquisite. The Dancing Ribbon needle is a punchneedle, and the way one uses it is a little different to the smaller types of punchneedle. The different action minimises potential damage to the fabric caused by punching the much larger diameter of the ribbon needle through the fabric.

SAFETY TIPS

Owing to its larger size and sharpness, the Dancing Ribbon Needle needs to be used with great care. It is also **very important** that the sharp needle tip is stored safely when not in use. When purchased, the sharp needle tip is housed inside the handle of the punchneedle for safety. I strongly suggest that when the Dancing Ribbon Needle is not in use you always replace the needle tip in the handle and securely tighten the nut. Care is also needed when working with the Dancing Ribbon needle, as the sharp tip extends quite some distance through the fabric.

   To remove the needle from the handle, hold the protruding blunt end, loosen the nut a few turns and fully remove the needle. Reverse the needle, carefully push the blunt end into the handle with the sharp tip protruding and tighten the nut to finger-tight at the needle length required.

Threading the Dancing Ribbon needle

The wire threader is inserted from the long side of the needle through the eye. Angle the threader, guide it into the bore of the needle and out through the handle. Thread the ribbon through the threader, and then slip the ribbon up into the small twist at the end of the threader where it will be held securely during threading. Leave only a small tag of ribbon. Gently pull the threader with the ribbon attached all the way through the handle and out through the eye of the needle.

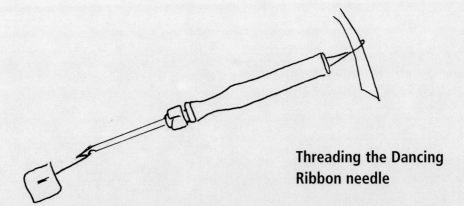

**Threading the Dancing
Ribbon needle**

Changing the length of the needle

Different sized loops can be made by changing the length of the needle. Simply loosen the nut, measure the required needle length as indicated in the design, then tighten the nut securely with your fingers.

Measuring the needle

Adjusting the loop length with the Dancing Ribbon needle is quite different to other punchneedles. Measure the needle from the tip to the nut and adjust accordingly. A ruler with no 'spare' on the end is ideal when measuring lengths for this needle (see ruler, page 53).

Using the Dancing Ribbon needle

Becasue the ribbons being worked with the Dancing Ribbon needle are wider than normal embroidery threads, the embroidery method is a little different to that of a regular punchneedle. Also, because of the thickness of the needle itself there is a risk of damaging some fabrics unless the following method is used.

Make sure the fabric is stretched tightly in the hoop. Place the needle tip at the point of insertion and guide it through the fabric with a gentle twisting action. This allows the tip to find its way between the fibres causing very little damage. The action is not like the punch-punch-punch of regular punchneedle work, but more a twist-in-lift-slide, twist-in-lift-slide action.

I suggest practising before starting this project. Remember, the tauter the fabric is in the hoop, the easier it is for the needle tip to find its way between the fibres. Once you have practised this form of embroidery fabulous results are possible. If fabric damage does occur, it may be that you will have to use a different fabric or fix an iron-on woven interfacing to the back of the fabric. The Dancing Ribbon needle will work easily through the added interfacing.

HANDY HINTS

◆ Hold the angled edge of the needle tip facing to the left if you are right-handed, and facing to the right if you are left-handed.

◆ Work from the back of the fabric, gently twisting the length of the needle through the fabric fully up to the handle. There is less chance of punching through loops already worked if the needle tip is angled slightly away from them.

◆ If there is too much resistance when using a particular ribbon or yarn, do not persist. Check the tightness of the fabric in the hoop or try a slightly narrower ribbon.

◆ When starting to embroider, hold the end tag of the ribbon on the back of the fabric to prevent the tag 'popping' through to the front of the fabric. Alternatively, tie a small knot at the very end of the ribbon, which prevents it escaping through to the front.

◆ Hold onto the ribbon loops made on the front as the needle tip is withdrawn from the fabric. If the ribbon is not held, the last loop may not stay in place. Holding the previously worked loops out of the way also prevents the Dancing Ribbon needle puncturing and damaging them. Work safely. Mind your fingers when you punch through again!

◆ There may be times when the loop on the front ends up with the ribbon doubled, not open to its full width. With your fingers, gently pull on each side of the loop to help it fully open. Some ribbons fold in half as they are pulled through the needle.

◆ Short loops are not so easy to open. If a loop isn't sitting well, the remedy may be as simple as turning the whole loop inside-out to allow it to open out more fully.

◆ To end, hold the ribbon in place with your index finger at the point of exit, then slide the punchneedle along the ribbon a little way before cutting and leaving a small tag.

Preparation

If using interfacing, iron it onto the back of one of the fabric squares, then trace the design onto the interfacing. Mark the two stems worked in reverse punchneedle embroidery (dotted lines) onto the front of the fabric with the water erasable pen.

If using interfacing, iron it onto the back of the second fabric square, on which three of the flowers will be embroidered. Mark the centre for the two big flowers (seen at the base of the arrangement) and the fallen flower, leaving enough space around each for the circles of fabric which will be cut out around them (see diagram 3).

Embroidery

TIP

It is not necessary to cut the ribbon at the end of each round. Simply pull the needle along the ribbon, set the new needle length and then pull the ribbon from the handle to tighten the ribbon again before beginning the next round

Gently open the ribbon loops as each round is completed.

Large cut-out flowers 1 and 2

See stitch guide for these flowers, and figure 23, Stitch Glossary.

Place the fabric, with flower centres marked, tautly in the hoop. Use the yellow 13 mm (½ in) silk ribbon.

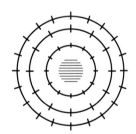

centre: 20 stitches
first round: 12 stitches
second round: 12 stitches
third round: 20 stitches

Stitch guide for cut-out flowers 1 and 2

Centres Measure the needle tip at 25 mm (1 in). Work 20 stitches in a circle.

See figure 6, Stitch Glossary, for a reminder on how to work in a circle: on the reverse side of the fabric gently guide the needle tip into the fabric leaving a tag of thread behind. Work very close to this tag. Work carefully around in a circle, in an outward spiral, pushing the tag out of the way. Punch as close to the tag as possible and work the number of stitches and rounds as indicated in the diagram, around in a circle. Where more than one round is to be worked to make up the circle,

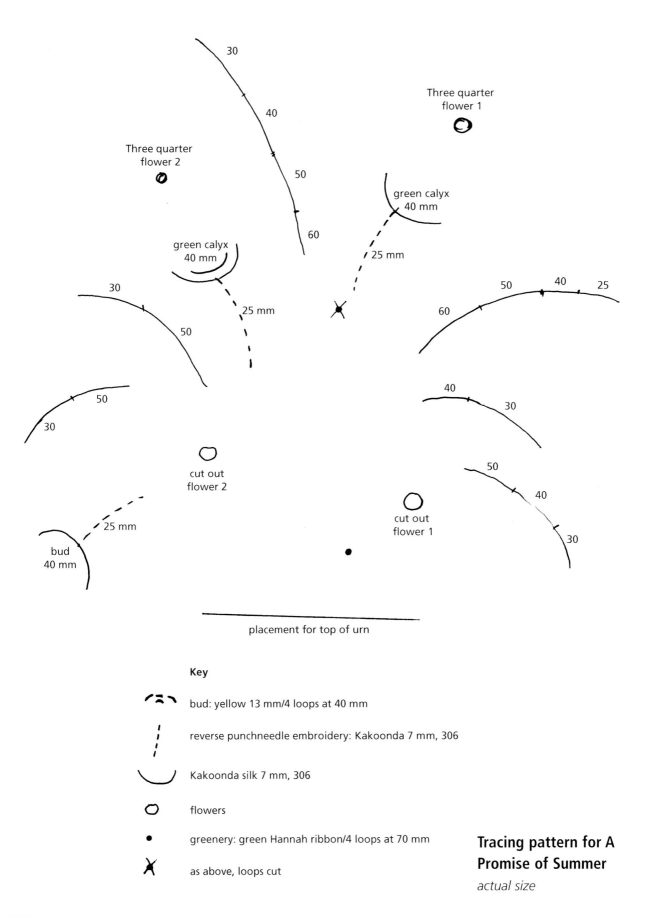

30

40

Three quarter
flower 1

50

Three quarter
flower 2

green calyx
40 mm

60

green calyx
40 mm

25 mm

30

50

50

40

25

50

60

25 mm

30

50

40

30

cut out
flower 2

50

40

cut out
flower 1

25 mm

30

bud
40 mm

placement for top of urn

Key

bud: yellow 13 mm/4 loops at 40 mm

reverse punchneedle embroidery: Kakoonda 7 mm, 306

Kakoonda silk 7 mm, 306

flowers

greenery: green Hannah ribbon/4 loops at 70 mm

as above, loops cut

**Tracing pattern for A
Promise of Summer**
actual size

draw a line with the water-erasable pen to show where the rounds start and end.

Leave the needle threaded when changing the measurements.

The petals First round: with the needle tip measured to 45 mm (approximately 1 ¾ in), embroider 12 stitches around the centre. Hold the ribbon in place as the needle is withdrawn. Draw the needle along the length of the ribbon about 12 cm (5 in) and lay the needle safely on the fabric in the hoop to allow room for measuring the needle tip for the next round to be worked. It is not necessary to cut the ribbon between each round.

Second round: with the needle tip measured to 60 mm (approximately 2 ⅓ in), work 2 mm (¹⁄₁₀ in) away from the first round and embroider 12 stitches around.

Third round: with the needle tip measured to 70 mm (approximately 2 ⅔ in), work 4 mm (⅕ in) away from the second round and embroider 20 stitches around. For this round the running stitch length on the back is about 4 mm (⅕ in).

Cut-out fallen flower

This flower is placed on the right side of the urn when the embroidery is completed.

Use yellow 7 mm (¼ in) silk ribbon.

Centre Measure the needle tip at 25 mm (1 in). Work 20 stitches.

Petals First round, with the needle tip measured to 30 mm (1 ¼ in), embroider 14 stitches around the centre.

Second round, with the needle tip measured to 40 mm (approximately 1 ½ in), work 2 mm (¹⁄₁₀ in) away from the first round, but this time only work three-quarters of the way around.

Finishing

Remove the fabric from the hoop.

Trim the ends of the flowers. Lightly glue over the back and leave to dry.

When dry, cut the fallen flower carefully away from the fabric, holding the long loops out of the way of the scissors.

Cut the fabric around flowers 1 and 2 in a circle as indicated on the cutting outline in diagram 3. With sewing needle and thread, run a small gathering stitch around the outside edge of the flower circle.

Place a small amount of wadding into the centre and pull the thread up tightly to form a small pad. The padded flowers add a further dimension to the finished embroidery.

Set these flowers aside.

Remaining embroidery

Place the fabric with the traced design tightly into the hoop with the design uppermost.

Mark the positions of the two three-quarter flowers on the main piece of fabric.

Three-quarter flower 1 is slightly larger than the other as it has 3 rounds of petals (see stitch guide for these flowers).

Flower 1
centre: 15 stitches
first round: 12 stitches
second round: 11 stitches
   three-quarters around circle
third round: 12 stitches
   three-quarters around circle

Flower 2
centre: 15 stitches
first round: 12 stitches
second round: 11 stitches
   three-quarters around circle
no third round

Stitch guide for three-quarter flowers

Three-quarter flower 1

Centre Measure the needle tip at 25 mm (1 in). Work 15 stitches in a circle.

Petals First round: with the needle tip measured to 45 mm (1 ¾ in), embroider 12 stitches around the centre.

Second round: with the needle tip measured to 55 mm (2 ¼ in), work 2 mm ($\frac{1}{10}$ in) away from the first round but only stitch three-quarters of the way around.

Third round: with the needle tip measured to 65 mm (approximately 2 ½ in), work 4 mm (approximately $\frac{1}{8}$ in) away from the second round, embroidering 11 stitches three-quarters of the way around.

Three-quarter flower 2

Work as above, but omit the third round.

Mauve spikes

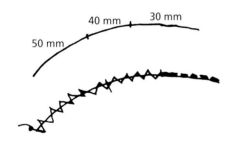

Diagram 1: Zigzag spike

See diagram 1, and figure 24, Stitch Glossary.

The spikes are embroidered in Kakoonda 13 mm (½ in) silk ribbon 3C. Follow the needle measurements and the lines for the spikes shown on the pattern. The longer loops nearer the middle of the design are worked not as a straight line but with a little zigzag (see the diagram). Measure the needle tip and change the length along the spikes as indicated.

Greenery

The three stems marked with dotted lines are worked in reverse punchneedle embroidery with 7 mm (¼ in) Kakoonda ribbon 306.

A calyx is worked under each three-quarter flower with the 7 mm green silk ribbon with needle tip measured at 40 mm (1 ⅛ in). A similar area is worked toward the bottom of the design on the left, where 4 loops of yellow 13 mm (½ in) silk ribbon are placed to resemble a bud, with needle tip measured at 50 mm (2 in). These areas are marked on the pattern.

There are two areas of leaves marked on the pattern with large black dots.

Diagram 2: Cutting points for greenery

The green Hannah silk ribbon is worked on the dots with the needle tip measured at 70 mm (approx. 2 ¾ in). The 4 loops in the middle of the flowers are cut into points (see diagram 2). The 4 loops below the flowers are not cut.

Finishing

Flowers 1 and 2 are stitched into place within the floral arrangement as indicated on the pattern, using a needle and thread. Position them so that they are angled a little with the centres facing to the sides, as in the photograph. Stitch firmly in place through the fabric backing of the flowers (which has been gathered and filled with a little padding; see diagram 3).

Trim any remaining ends of the ribbon on the back of the piece and fix in place with a tiny

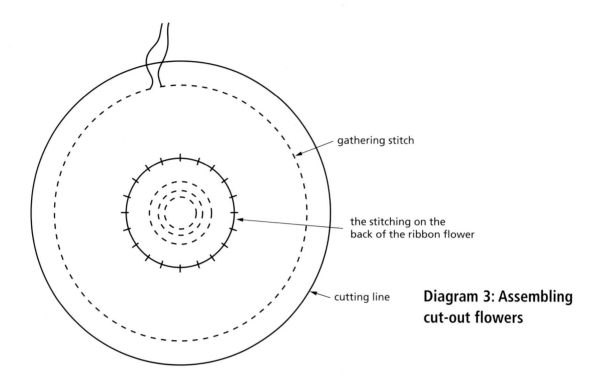

gathering stitch

the stitching on the
back of the ribbon flower

cutting line

**Diagram 3: Assembling
cut-out flowers**

amount of You Can Wash It craft glue.

Remove the work from the hoop and carefully press around the outside of the embroidery. Stitch the separate piece of base fabric loosely below the main flower arrangement, manipulating it into appealing folds before attaching it. Trim it to the same size as the base fabric.

Glue the urn in place, pushing it up under the looped leaves so that they can flow over the top.

Glue or stitch the fallen flower into place at the side of the urn.

Frame appropriately and enjoy!!

Framing

Silk ribbon projects require a built-up box frame to prevent the glass squashing the loops. Place some wadding or pellon behind the finished piece before framing to provide more shape and interest.

Gallery

using various techniques achieved simply with punchneedle embroidery to give undulations and mossy areas. The leaves are all handmade and have been scattered over the work along with found objects.

Bush Cocktail

The background is painted calico with the texture being added using the technique of punchneedle embroidery. Thirty-seven colours of six-stranded embroidery cotton have been used to interpret the Australian bush colours, leaves and insects.

Kandinski Sails on Silver

A boat-like structure with miniature punchneedle embroideries set into sterling silver sails. Inspired by and interpreted from a painting by the artist Vasily Kandinsky (1866–1944), using colours similar to his artwork. The miniature sails have been worked using a very fine punchneedle with one strand of thread.

Bush Floor

The technique of punchneedle embroidery is perfect for creating highly textured embroidery. Worked with six strands of embroidery cotton, the Australian bush floor has been interpreted

A Rock in a Silver Space

A miniature sculpture of Uluru (Ayers Rock) worked with one strand of thread through a very fine punchneedle. There are approximately 450 stitches worked in each square centimetre of the embroidery, which is suspended in an unpolished sterling silver frame.

Bracelet

A visually exciting piece of wearable art. A chunky designer-made sterling silver structure which houses a miniature embroidery.

The Gum Leaf

In this piece I have attempted to capture all the colours seen in a leaf found on one of my daily walks. An interpretation of a gum leaf using many blended colours and one strand of thread with the technique of punchneedle embroidery. Approximately 350 stitches to the square centimetre.

Silver Pendant

A miniature punchneedle embroidery set into a designer-made sterling silver surround. Single strands of embroidery thread forming more than 500 stitches have been worked around a tiny sterling silver bead. A twenty-first birthday present for my daughter.

Suppliers

Other publications by Pamela Gurney:

Punchneedle Embroidery (1997), 5 Mile Press (out of print)

Punch Crazy (1999), Aussie Publishers

Video *Punchneedle Embroidery*

For the book *Punch Crazy* and the video, available in NTSC & VHS, contact Pamela Gurney at:

Dancing Needle Designs

Supplier of all supplies necessary for punchneedle embroidery: punchneedles, books, threads, ribbons, fabric, terracotta pots and pattern packs and kits.

PO Box 302

Kangaroo Ground, Vic 3097, Australia

email: pamela@dancingneedles.com

web: www.punchneedleembroidery.com and www.dancingneedles.com

Products by Cameo, Inc

Suppliers of punchneedles and acrylic yarn

2573–DN Forshyth Rd

Orlando

Florida 32807 USA

tel: (407) 677-1139

fax: (407) 671-7098

Pretty Products of America, Inc

Suppliers of acrylic yarn

PO Box 13087

Scottsdale, AZ 85267 USA

Madeira Threads

Suppliers of cotton embroidery thread

SSS Pty Ltd

16 Valediction Rd

Kings Park, NSW 2148, Australia

tel: 61 2 9672 3888

Madeira Threads USA (headquarters)

30 Bayside Court (PO Box 6068)

Laconia NH 03246 USA

800 225 3001

tel: 603 528 2944

fax: 603 528 4264

email: Madeirausa@aol.com

Rajmahal Threads Australia

Suppliers of art silks and satin-covered boxes

182 High Street

Kangaroo Flat, Vic 3555, Australia

tel: 61 3 5447 7699

fax: 61 3 5447 7899

email: rajinfo@ozemail.com.au

web: http://www.rajmahal.com.au

Kakoonda

Suppliers of hand-dyed silk ribbon

PO Box 4073

Langwarrin Vic 3910 Australia

Craftsmart

Suppliers of You Can Wash It and On'N'Off craft glues and Fray Stop

4/29 Business Park Drive

Nottinghill Vic 3168 Australia

The little wooden stool (Overflowing Cornucopia) is available from specialist craft shops.

Bunka Yarn

Kléma

Unit 3A/1 High Rd

Bethania, Qld 4205, Australia

Necessity Notions

Ben Britim Distributors Pty Ltd

'Vailima'

Scarlett St

Mittagong, NSW 2575, Australia